ALTMAN, M.

A TASTE OF
SMALLTALK

A TASTE OF SMALLTALK

Seeing is deceiving
It's eating that's believing

JAMES THURBER

TED KAEHLER

Xerox PARC and Apple

DAVE PATTERSON

University of California, Berkeley

W · W · NORTON & COMPANY · NEW YORK · LONDON

FIRST EDITION

ISBN 0-393-95505-2

W. W. Norton & Company, Inc.,
500 Fifth Avenue, New York, N. Y. 10110
W. W. Norton & Company Ltd.,
37 Great Russell Street, London WC1B 3NU

1 2 3 4 5 6 7 8 9 0

CONTENTS

PREFACE

THE BOOK

The Smalltalk-80™ system* is both a civilized programming environment and the premier "object-oriented" programming language. The programming environment offers an elegant and highly integrated set of tools: overlapping windows on a diverse set of applications appear together on the screen, and a single button click moves the user from one application to another. The system makes it easy to search, view code, edit, detect syntax errors, and execute code, all from within a single window. As a language, Smalltalk offers a uniform and powerful metaphor: procedures and data that belong together are packaged in an "object." An object interacts with the rest of the system by singling out another object and sending it a message. Smalltalk's combination of good editors, a natural modularization of code, and a language based on a powerful idea forms a system that is at its best during the construction and evolution of a large applications program.

A new programming system is enticing to most programmers, especially when it promises increased productivity. Alas, this enthusiasm wanes when the programmer confronts the mountain of documentation that must be conquered before writing a first, simple program. The dilemma is compounded when the new system uses terms and ideas that are unlike any encountered before. The delightfully slothful

---

*Smalltalk-80 is a registered trademark of the Xerox Corporation. In other corporate news, UNIX is a trademark of AT&T, VAX is a trademark of Digital Equipment, SUN is a trademark of Sun Microsystems, IBM is a trademark of International Business Machines Corp., and Macintosh is a trademark licensed to Apple Computer, Inc.

programmer generally looks for friends to guide him. Without such guides, the programmer returns to the old familiar programming environment, feeling secure, if slightly disappointed.

We must confess that this insight comes from personal experience and not from scholarly observation. When students at the University of California at Berkeley first confronted a working Smalltalk-80 system, they found that they didn't know what to do next. Although they knew a lot about the Smalltalk language and its user interface, they didn't know where to begin. We wrote this book to tell them, and to provide a gentle introduction to Smalltalk for the well-adjusted slothful programmer. We suspect that there are many people of kindred spirit who want to learn the Smalltalk-80 system—perhaps even you.

The purpose of this tutorial is to give you a taste of programming in the Smalltalk-80 language and environment. Our approach is to guide you through several versions of a small program in a short time. If these small examples get you interested, then larger programs will get you addicted, for the power of the Smalltalk-80 system increases as programs grow.

We introduce the system a piece at a time, taking as our example your favorite recursive program, the Tower of Hanoi, and giving complete programs with explanations. Rather than starting from first principles, we use the "Rosetta Stone" approach: in Chapter 1, we show Pascal, C, and LISP versions (it will help if you know one of these languages), and then present a Smalltalk version for comparison. The next three chapters show how to enhance the program and turn it into a Smalltalk class. Along the way we tour several parts of the Smalltalk-80 system that will be useful in other applications. In Chapter 5, we'll spice up the program by making the disks fly between the towers on the graphics display, while in Chapter 6 we depart from the standard recursive solution and present a heuristic algorithm, which nevertheless uses our original data structures to solve the puzzle. Through rewriting the Tower of Hanoi program we demonstrate the value of "object-oriented" programming and show how the proper use of objects can make a program intuitive and easy to modify.

We assume you know how to program and have seen how the mouse interacts with windows on a bit-mapped display. This tutorial is best if you have a Smalltalk-80 system to try it on. The book is also valuable if you don't have access to a running system but just want to find out what Smalltalk is really like. To give you a feeling for Smalltalk, the system, we have included many pictures of the screen. By using this book with any of several commercially available Smalltalk-80 systems, you can write an interactive, graphical Smalltalk program in a day or less. You will then be in a better position to decide if you want to learn more about Smalltalk, and, perhaps more significant, you can amaze your programming friends with phrases like, "Well, I've *written* a Smalltalk-80 program, and I think . . ."

RELATIONSHIP TO THE SMALLTALK REFERENCE MANUALS

Some books are to be tasted,
others to be swallowed,
and some few to be chewed and digested.
FRANCIS BACON, *Of Studies*

1983 was a landmark year in Smalltalk's history, as the number of Smalltalk books went from zero to three. The first book, *Smalltalk-80: The Language and Its Implementation*, by Adele Goldberg and David Robson (Reading, Massachusetts: Addison-Wesley, 1983), plays such an important role that we will refer to it as the "Blue Book." It describes the language and interpreter in detail, thereby defining the Smalltalk-80 language. In addition, the Blue Book gives an example of the design and implementation of a moderate-sized program.

Smalltalk-80: The Interactive Programming Environment, by Adele Goldberg (Reading, Massachusetts: Addison-Wesley, 1984), documents the manner in which Smalltalk presents itself on the screen. It catalogs and explains the various windows, menus, and editors in the Smalltalk-80 programming environment, and what the user must do to run them. We refer to it as the "User's Guide."

Glenn Krasner edited *Smalltalk-80: Bits of History, Words of Advice* (Reading, Massachusetts: Addison-Wesley, 1983), a collection of papers describing several implementations of Smalltalk. His book is for people interested in building Smalltalk-80 systems, and is not intended for those who only want to use such systems.

In contrast to these titles, *A Taste of Smalltalk* does not tackle the syntax and semantics of the language head-on, but eases you into the Smalltalk system by translating a familiar program from another language. The example is then expanded to show off the interactive nature of the system. In short, this book is for programmers who want to build some example programs in Smalltalk with as little preparation as possible.

A LANGUAGE AND AN ENVIRONMENT

The Smalltalk language is based on a small number of consistent abstractions. Like LISP, Smalltalk seeks to provide uniform treatment of different kinds of information—text, graphics, symbols, and numbers. By packaging the behavior of each form of information with the actual data, the information can be shared between programs without changing representations. Often, code is general enough to be "reused," reducing the size of programs.

The source code for every part of the Smalltalk-80 system is available in **System Browser** windows. A Smalltalk programmer typically uses an editor to build upon an existing part of the system by modification. Overlapping windows make it possible to see several pieces of your code and several pieces of system code at once while you are debugging (Smalltalk was the first system to allow users to do this).

Smalltalk is an exploratory system, in which it is easy to make changes and test prototypes. Pieces of Smalltalk code tend to be small; they are compiled incrementally and take effect instantly. Such a system invites capricious change, which often leads to innovation and improvement. The goal is to provide an environment in which you can take a fall and get up again faster than you could plan a careful, conservative course of action. The text editor and many other parts of the Smalltalk-80 system were built from within the running system—an exhilarating and surprisingly safe experience. Smalltalk is at its best in large applications. The tools and editors are ideal for the frequent changes that are necessary in large software projects.

SMALLTALK ROOTS

Smalltalk was developed in the Learning Research Group at Xerox's Palo Alto Research Center in the early 1970s. The major ideas in Smalltalk belong to Alan Kay, who traces their roots to Simula, LISP, and SketchPad. Early implementations were masterminded by Dan Ingalls (the first person to write code for multiple overlapping windows, opaque pop-up menus, and BitBlt*). 1972 to 1979 were Smalltalk's formative years, and the Smalltalk-80 system is a "presentable" and documented version of Smalltalk-76.

Smalltalk runs on a personal computer with a high-resolution display and a pointing device. While the language is fairly concise, the environment is rather large, though not nearly as large as UNIX™.

---

*BitBlt, also called "raster-op," is a general-purpose operation for moving rectangles of bits from any position to any other position on a bit-mapped display.

Smalltalk has taxed every machine on which it has run, including Xerox Altos, VAXes, SUNs, and Xerox Dorados, but the recent growth in power and speed of microcomputers has made it practical to implement Smalltalk on low-cost machines. From engineering workstations Smalltalk has spread to increasingly inexpensive personal computers. The vendors offering Smalltalk-80 systems as of January 1986 are given in the table below.

Machine	Where to Get the Software	License
Xerox 1100, 1108x, 1132	Xerox	2
Tektronix 4404, 4405, 4406	Tektronix	2
Sun 2	U.C. Berkeley*	2
IBM PC AT	Softsmarts, Inc.**	2
Apple Macintosh 1MB	Apple***	1 (Level 1)
Apple Macintosh 512K	Apple	1 (Level 0)

*Berkeley distributes an interpreter written in C that runs under UNIX. Before you can buy Berkeley's interpreter, you must obtain a license for the Smalltalk-80 system from Xerox.

**In case you haven't heard of them, Softsmarts, Incorporated is located in Woodside, California. They offer the genuine License 2 Smalltalk-80 system from Xerox on an IBM PC AT.

***The Apple Level 1 Smalltalk system runs on a Macintosh Plus, a Macintosh that has been upgraded to 1MB, or a Macintosh XL running MacWorks. The Apple Level 1 and Level 0 systems are available from Apple as unsupported releases and are not official products as of this writing.

Two different versions of the Smalltalk-80 system are licensed by Xerox. License 2 is the standard system documented in the reference manuals, and is the system that Xerox is actively licensing to computer manufacturers and universities. License 1 is an older system that is available from Apple. *A Taste of Smalltalk* primarily describes License 2 systems, but does include instructions for using License 1 systems whenever possible.

ACKNOWLEDGMENTS

We wish to thank all the members of the System Concepts Laboratory at the Xerox Palo Alto Research Center. Adele Goldberg and Dave Robson wrote the reference manuals for Smalltalk, and we could not have written this without their previous work. We wish to thank Alan Kay and especially Dan Ingalls for their gift to the world, which we celebrate in this book. Students at Berkeley who worked on Smalltalk provided inspiration. The following people, listed alphabetically, tested the tutorial and gave us valuable feedback: Bill Baldwin, Ron

Clockwise from above: The complete
License 2 version of Smalltalk-80 running
on the IBM PC AT (photo courtesy of
Softsmarts, Inc.); a 512K Macintosh with
one disk drive running Apple's Level 0
Smalltalk system (photo by Mark Embury,
Palo Alto, California); Smalltalk-80 on the
Tektronix 4404 Artificial Intelligence System
(photo courtesy of Tektronix, Inc.).

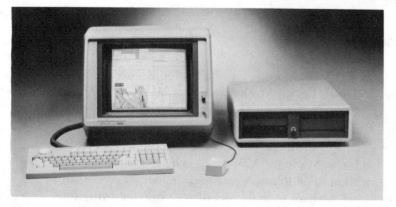

Carter, Yuchee Chen, Jeanetta Cooper, Bill Croca, Al Hoffman, Peter K. Lee, Mark Lentczner, Frank Ludolph, Randy Smith, and Marvin Zauderer. Lissy Bland wrote an early version of the answers to the exercises, and Mark Lentczner wrote the programs that answered a later version. Adele Goldberg, Glenn Krasner, Larry Tesler, SueAnn Ambron, and Carol Kaehler reviewed the manuscript and made many vital suggestions. Todd MacMillan provided technical assistance. We also thank John Hawkins of W. W. Norton for his profoundly steadying influence on this project. Carol Kaehler (the real writer in one family) and Linda Patterson (the real artist in the other) provided inspiration, and this book is dedicated to them.

A TASTE OF
SMALLTALK

THE EXAMPLE

THE TOWER OF HANOI

RECURSIVE: adj. see RECURSIVE.
STAN KELLY-BOOTLE, *Devil's DP Dictionary*

This program represents one of the few examples of agreement in computer science. Practically every programming text introduces recursion using this program, and, in this case, Smalltalk is no exception. The Tower of Hanoi is based on a game (popular in the 1960s) that had its own mythology (also popular in the 1960s):

An ancient myth has it that in some temple in the Far East, time is marked off by monks engaged in the transfer of 64 disks from one of three pins to another. The universe as we know it will end when they are done. The reason we do not have to concern ourselves about the cosmological implications of this is that their progress is kept in check by some clever rules: the monks can only move one disk at a time; the disks all have different diameters; and no disk can ever be placed on top of a smaller one.*

---

* P.H. Winston and B.K.P. Horn, *LISP* (Reading, Massachusetts: Addison-Wesley Publishing Company, 1981), 88.

The rules seem easy enough, except with 64 disks you might get a little confused and never be sure if you were making forward progress. Luckily, there is a way to simplify things and find an algorithm. We quote from the second edition of *Oh! Pascal!* by Doug Cooper and Michael Clancy.

Let's try to get a handle on how the moves are made for stacks of various heights. Clearly a height of 1 is trivial—we move the disk directly from A to C. What about a height of 2? We put the top disk out of the way—to B. Then the bottom disk goes to C, and the smaller disk from B to C.

With a stack of height 3 it gets interesting. Let's suppose, though, that we restate the problem (as we're liable to do when we're up to something). Instead of moving 3 disks from A to C, let's move 2 disks from A to B—we already know how to move two disks from one peg to another. Next, move the third disk directly to C. Finally, make another two-disk move, from B to C. We've switched all three disks.

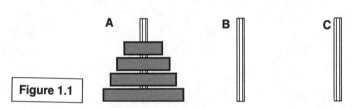

Figure 1.1

How about starting with 4 disks? [See Figure 1.1.] Once more, let's begin by restating the problem. Can we move 3 disks from A to B? Sure—it's essentially the same as moving them from A to C. [See Figure 1.2.]

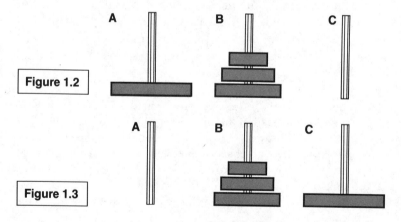

Figure 1.2

Figure 1.3

Then we switch the fourth disk directly from A to C [Figure 1.3], and, finally, transfer 3 disks from B to C. [See Figure 1.4.]

As you can probably gather, we've insisted on restating the problem in a particular way each time so that we can develop a special insight. We

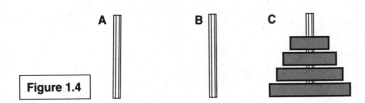

Figure 1.4

begin to solve the Towers of Hanoi problem for a stack of height n by trying to solve it for a stack of height $n-1$. This solution must wait until we solve for $(n-1)-1$, and so on. Eventually we get to the trivial case of n equaling 1, and can begin to work our way back up.

Almost without realizing it, we've used a high-priced method of thinking called *induction*. We start by solving a simple case of the Towers of Hanoi problem—a tower of height one or two. Then, we show that even if we start with a larger number, we can always work our way down to a problem that we know how to solve. This is the heart of what will become our recursive solution to the problem.

Now we're ready to make a recursive statement of our solution. To move n disks from peg A to peg C:
1. Move $n-1$ disks from A to B.
2. Move 1 disk from A to C.
3. Move $n-1$ disks from B to C.
In steps 1 and 3, of course, we will use the remaining peg as an auxiliary "holding" peg.*

Versions of this algorithm in Pascal, C, LISP, and Smalltalk are shown on the next pages. In the programs "frompin" refers to the index of the pin a disk will move from, "topin" refers to its destination, and "usingpin" refers to the remaining pin. To describe the poles that hold the disks, we will use the word "pole" in the text and "pin" in the programs. We were surprised at the variety of notation for the same program in the three "normal" programming languages.

A ROSETTA STONE: PASCAL, C, LISP, AND SMALLTALK

The Tower of Hanoi in Pascal

This program is derived from a program found on pages 102–103 in *Programming in Pascal* by Peter Grogono, Addison-Wesley, Reading, Massachusetts, 1978.

---

* Doug Cooper and Michael Clancy, *Oh! Pascal!*, 2nd edition (New York: Norton, 1985), 237–38.

```
program hanoi(input, output);
    var total : integer;

    procedure movetower (Height, Frompin, Topin, Usingpin : integer);

        procedure movedisk ( Frompin, Topin : integer);
        begin
                writeln( Frompin, ' ->', Topin)
        end; { movedisk }

    begin { movetower }
        if Height > 0 then
            begin
                movetower(Height - 1, Frompin, Usingpin, Topin);
                movedisk( Frompin, Topin);
                movetower(Height - 1, Usingpin, Topin, Frompin)
            end
    end; { movetower }

begin { hanoi }
    read(total);
    movetower(total, 1, 3, 2)
end. { hanoi }
```

If you wanted to run the program on Berkeley Unix 4.2 on the VAX-11/780, you would type the above program into hanoi.p and then type:

> *pix hanoi.p*

(which compiles and interprets the program). It replies with:

> *Execution begins.* . .

You now type the number of disks:

> *3*

and here is what happens:

1 ->	*3*
1 ->	*2*
3 ->	*2*
1 ->	*3*
2 ->	*1*
2 ->	*3*
1 ->	*3*

and at the end of the program the Pascal interpreter types:

> *Execution terminated.*
>
> *45 statements executed in 0.05 seconds cpu time.*

The Tower of Hanoi in C

Here is a C version to examine:

```
main()
{
  int howmany;
  howmany = getchar() - '0';
  movetower(howmany,1,3,2);
}

movetower(height,frompin,topin,usingpin)
int height,frompin,topin,usingpin;
{
  if(height > 0) {
    /* Move the whole stack on frompin to usingpin */
    movetower(height-1,frompin,usingpin,topin);
    /* Move the bottom disk */
    movedisk(frompin,topin);
    /* Move the whole stack on usingpin to topin */
    movetower(height-1,usingpin,topin,frompin);
  };
}

movedisk(frompin,topin) int frompin,topin;
{
    printf("%d -> %d\n",frompin,topin);
}
```

If you wanted to run the program on Berkeley Unix 4.2 on the
VAX-11/780, you would type the above program into hanoi.c and then
type:

    cc hanoi.c

(which compiles the program). You then type

    a.out

(the name of the object file) and then you type the number of disks:

    3

and here is what happens:

       1 -> 3
       1 -> 2
       3 -> 2
       1 -> 3
       2 -> 1
       2 -> 3
       1 -> 3

The Tower of Hanoi in LISP

This program is derived from a program found on pages 88-90 in *LISP* by P.H. Winston and B.K.P. Horn, Addison-Wesley, Reading, Massachusetts, 1981.

```
(defun Tower-Of-Hanoi nil (Transfer '1 '3 '2 (read)))    ; N disks on 1 first.
(defun Move-Disk (From-pin To-pin)
     (print (list From-pin ' - > To-pin))                ; Print instruction.
     (terpri))                                           ; Start new line.
(defun Transfer (From-pin To-pin Using-pin Height)
     (cond ((equal Height 1)
       (Move-Disk From-pin To-pin))                      ; Transfer one disk.
     (t (Transfer   From-pin                             ; Move from From-pin
         Using-pin                                        ; to Using-pin
         To-pin                                           ; using To-pin as space
         (sub1 Height))                                   ; (n - 1) disks.
       (Move-Disk From-pin To-pin)                        ; Move lowest disk.
       (Transfer   Using-pin                              ; Move from Using-pin
         To-pin                                           ; to To-pin
         From-pin                                         ; using From-pin as space
         (sub1 Height)))))                                ; (n - 1) disks.
```

If you wanted to run the program on Berkeley Unix 4.2 on the VAX-11/780, you would type the above program into hanoi.lisp and then type:
> *lisp*

It replies with:
> *Franz Lisp, Opus 38.72*
> − >

You now load the program:
> *(load 'hanoi.lisp)*

and it replies with:
> *[load hanoi.lisp]*
> *t*

To invoke the program you type:
> *(Tower-Of-Hanoi)*

then tell it the number of disks:
> *3*

and here is what happens:
     (1 —> 3)
     (1 —> 2)
     (3 —> 2)
     (1 —> 3)
     (2 —> 1)
     (2 —> 3)
     (1 —> 3)
     nil
You then type *control D* and it says:
     Goodbye

The Tower of Hanoi in Smalltalk

In the Smalltalk version of the program, there are two procedures. Each is typed separately into the bottom pane of a window on the screen (called the **System Browser**) and then compiled and merged into the system by choosing a command from a pop-up menu. (Don't try to type this in now. If you absolutely can't stand not running the Smalltalk version now, you may skip to the second section of Chapter 2, and continue on into Chapter 3.)

```
moveTower: height from: fromPin to: toPin using: usingPin
    "Recursive procedure to move the disk at a height from one
    pin to another pin using a third pin"
    (height > 0) ifTrue: [
        self moveTower: (height – 1) from: fromPin to: usingPin using: toPin.
        self moveDisk: fromPin to: toPin.
        self moveTower: (height – 1) from: usingPin to: toPin using: fromPin]
```

```
moveDisk: fromPin to: toPin
    "Move disk from a pin to another pin. Print the results in the
    transcript window"
    Transcript cr.
    Transcript show: (fromPin printString, ' –> ', toPin printString).
```

To run the program, type the text given below into any window that can contain Smalltalk code, select it, and choose **do it** from the middle-button pop-up menu.

```
(Object new) moveTower: 3 from: 1 to: 3 using: 2.
```

The **Transcript Window** will show:

```
1 -> 3
1 -> 2
3 -> 2
1 -> 3
2 -> 1
2 -> 3
1 -> 3
```

We chose the Tower of Hanoi as an example because it is a short program that solves an interesting problem, and because it is so widely used. However, we are astonished at how unclear this recursive solution is. The program has no permanent variables and no assignment statements. The "movedisk" routine does not actually move anything. If you stop the program in the middle, where is the information stored? Generations of students have been confused by the fact that the entire state of the towers is held "on the stack." The arguments to all of the "movetower" routines that are suspended, partially finished, hold the information about the locations of the disks.

The recursive solution presented here is not "object-oriented." The program in Smalltalk looks very much like the program in the other languages. It contains objects, but they are not exhibiting the full power of object-oriented programming. In Chapter 6, we will explore a more intuitive algorithm for solving the Tower of Hanoi problem. The Smalltalk program we write for it will show off objects and object-oriented programming to their full advantage.

Let's face it, except for all those parentheses in one language (we won't point fingers), and all those colons in another, there isn't much difference between the programs. Smalltalk, however, has an unconventional model underneath that belies its surface similarity to other languages.

Messages and Objects Everywhere

THE SMALLTALK-80 LANGUAGE

When I use a word, . . .
it means just what I choose it to mean
— neither more nor less.
LEWIS CARROLL, *Alice's Adventures in Wonderland*

Smalltalk strives to use a small number of consistent abstractions and terms, unconstrained by conventions or terms from other programming languages. For example, a Smalltalk procedure or subroutine is called a "method." We will try to justify the Smalltalk names as soon as you learn enough to understand the excuse, but for now we will keep the unconventional names to a minimum in this tutorial. Generally we will give the Smalltalk name with the conventional name in parentheses, or vice versa. Variable names in Smalltalk are often highly descriptive, and thus quite long. Following the Smalltalk tradition, we use capitals as visual separators (moveTower) instead of hyphens (move-tower). In the next few paragraphs we explain Smalltalk relying mainly on Pascal terminology, with four figures highlighting different aspects of the moveTower procedure.

The "moveTower" procedure has local names for its arguments, and these are underlined below. All text that is between double quotes is a comment (comments are shown in italics in this chapter only). It is surprising that four languages have four different notations for something as simple as a comment. Next is an expression, (height > 0), that evaluates to true or false. The Smalltalk if-statement is like Pascal except that the Boolean expression precedes, instead of follows, the "if." Next is a block, similar to the C curly bracket notation, except that Smalltalk surrounds blocks with square brackets. There is a comment at the end of the procedure.

```
moveTower: height from: fromPin to: toPin using: usingPin
  "Recursive procedure to move the disk at a height from one
  pin to another pin using a third pin"
  (height > 0) ifTrue: [
    self moveTower: (height − 1) from: fromPin to: usingPin using: toPin.
    self moveDisk: fromPin to: toPin.
    self moveTower: (height − 1) from: usingPin to: toPin using: fromPin]


  "This comment gives an example of how to run this program. Select
  the following and choose 'do it' from the middle-button menu.
  (Object new) moveTower: 3 from: 1 to: 3 using: 2        "
```

In Smalltalk, periods are used to separate statements. Pascal and C programmers will find this syntax familiar provided they remember to use '.' instead of ';'. There are three statements in the block, shown in boxes below, and they are executed sequentially.

```
moveTower: height from: fromPin to: toPin using: usingPin
  "Recursive procedure to move the disk at a height from one
  pin to another pin using a third pin"
  (height > 0) ifTrue: [
```

| self moveTower: (height − 1) from: fromPin to: usingPin using: toPin. |
| self moveDisk: fromPin to: toPin. |
| self moveTower: (height − 1) from: usingPin to: toPin using: fromPin |]

```
  "This comment gives an example of how to run this program. Select
  the following and choose 'do it' from the middle-button menu.
  (Object new) moveTower: 3 from: 1 to: 3 using: 2        "
```

The designers of the Smalltalk language chose a format for procedure names that encourages the programmer to describe each of the arguments. The idea is to provide more than just the order of the arguments to help the programmer remember which one is which. Each part of a procedure name ends with a colon and is followed by the argument it describes. This notation could be used in any language.

The four underlined words in the first line below are the four parts of the name of the procedure (method) that is being defined. When you want to talk about the procedure, squeeze all the parts of its name together; in this example, the actual name of the procedure we have been working with is moveTower:from:to:using:. It has four arguments and corresponds to the Pascal procedure named "movetower." This procedure calls three procedures (itself twice and moveDisk:to: once) and those names are also underlined. The interleaving of pieces of procedure names with the arguments is just syntactic sugar, and you may find it useful to translate calls on this procedure to the familiar format of procedure name followed by arguments:

moveTower:from:to:using: (height, fromPin, toPin, usingPin).

```
moveTower: height from: fromPin to: toPin using: usingPin
    "Recursive procedure to move the disk at a height from one
    pin to another pin using a third pin"
    (height > 0) ifTrue: [
        self moveTower: (height − 1) from: fromPin to: usingPin using: toPin.
        self moveDisk: fromPin to: toPin.
        self moveTower: (height − 1) from: usingPin to: toPin using: fromPin]

    "This comment gives an example of how to run this program. Select
    the following and choose 'do it' from the middle-button menu.
    (Object new) moveTower: 3 from: 1 to: 3 using: 2        "
```

As mentioned above, Smalltalk strives for consistent abstractions. While most languages treat operators and procedure names as separate entities, Smalltalk lumps them together, calling them "message selectors." Both > and moveTower:from:to:using: are message selectors.

You've probably heard that Smalltalk is an object-oriented system, and may be curious to know what an "object" is. An object is a package of data and procedures that belong together. Specifically, all constants and the contents of all variables are objects. An object in Smalltalk is like a record in Pascal, but much richer and more versatile. Below, we have underlined all the objects in our example. The only things that don't denote objects are the message selectors (operators or procedure names), the comments, and a few punctuation characters.

```
moveTower: height from: fromPin to: toPin using: usingPin
    "Recursive procedure to move the disk at a height from one
    pin to another pin using a third pin"
    (height > 0) ifTrue: [
        self moveTower: (height − 1) from: fromPin to: usingPin using: toPin.
        self moveDisk: fromPin to: toPin.
        self moveTower: (height − 1) from: usingPin to: toPin using: fromPin]
```

"This comment gives an example of how to run this program. Select
the following and choose 'do it' from the middle-button menu.
(Object new) moveTower: 3 from: 1 to: 3 using: 2   *"*

Most systems get work done in a variety of ways: by calling procedures, applying operators to operands, conditionally executing blocks, and so forth. Following the goal of using a small number of consistent abstractions, Smalltalk has exactly one way of getting work done: by "sending messages" to objects. A message is just an operator or procedure name (message selector) with its operands. The object that receives a message, the "receiver," appears just to the left of the message. We have boxed some of the messages in the code below.

```
moveTower: height from: fromPin to: toPin using: usingPin
    "Recursive procedure to move the disk at a height from one
    pin to another pin using a third pin"
    (height > 0 ) ifTrue: [
        self moveTower: (height −1 ) from: fromPin to: usingPin using: toPin .
        self moveDisk: fromPin to: toPin .
        self moveTower: (height −1 ) from: usingPin to: toPin using: fromPin ]
```

"This comment gives an example of how to run this program. Select
the following and choose 'do it' from the middle-button menu.
(Object new) moveTower: 3 from: 1 to: 3 using: 2   *"*

Smalltalk always returns a value as the result of each procedure (method), and, as you might expect from an object-oriented language, that result is also an object. For example, height − 1 returns an integer and height > 0 returns a boolean.

You now know enough that we can explain more Smalltalk lingo. The terms "method" (procedure) and "selector" (procedure name) come from the question, "How do we *select* the *method* an object will use to respond to this message?" The answer is, "Use the *selector* to find the right *method* to execute." A message is just the operator or procedure name (message selector) along with its arguments. "Calling a procedure" is translated in Smalltalkese as "sending a message." From now on, we will use the term "method" instead of "procedure" or "subroutine."

If you talk to yourself while you read code (don't be bashful, everyone does), then you need to know how to "talk" Smalltalk. **height > 0** does exactly what you think it does, and you can pronounce it just the way you would in other languages ("height is greater than zero"); but it is really shorthand for "the object height receives the message greater-than with the argument zero." For the really dedicated code talkers, see Appendix 2. We will sprinkle Smalltalkese throughout this tutorial, but you can survive this experience without learning the complete dialect.

The object-message paradigm is natural for simulation programs. For example, sending the message **throttleOpen: 30** to the object that is simulating an automobile engine might mean that the gas pedal is pressed to 30 percent of maximum. When an object receives a message, it looks up the message name to see if it understands the message. If the message is found, it starts executing the "method" that tells how to respond to the message.

Just as a Pascal procedure may call other procedures, a method may need to call other methods. The way to start another method is to send a message to an object. Sometimes you want to send a message to the same object that received the current message. How is that object named locally? In other words, when a Smalltalk object talks to itself, what does it call itself? Why, "self," naturally! Not surprisingly, messages to **self** are common. You can see them sprinkled throughout the program on the previous page. How does Smalltalk handle recursion? In Pascal, the definition of a procedure can include a call on itself. In Smalltalk, the code within a method sends a mesage to the object **self**, in particular, a message with the same selector as the current method.

Specifying an object, sending it a message, and getting back another object as the result are the only things that ever happen in Smalltalk code. Things that require new kinds of constructs in other languages, such as control structures and arithmetic operators, are simply messages sent to objects in Smalltalk. The result of one message can be used as the object that receives another message, or as an argument in another message. For example, the object that is the result of the message **− 1** being sent to **height** is used in each of these ways in **moveTower:from:to:using:**. Except for the assignment operator (covered in the next chapter), all Smalltalk code is a grand concoction of messages sent to objects.

DEFINING A METHOD

For those that like this sort of thing,
this is the sort of thing they like.

MAX BEERBOHM

The best way to read this section is while sitting in front of a Smalltalk-80 system. (But we supply lots of pictures to help readers who have only an imaginary Smalltalk machine.) Notice that Smalltalk relies on a bit-mapped graphic display and pointing device, rather than a conventional character-oriented display. This difference means little to the Smalltalk language, but a large screen makes programming much easier than on a traditional display terminal. Seeing more than one piece of code at a time relieves a large mental burden.

It will probably save you time if you get a friend to show you how to start Smalltalk, move the mouse, use the mouse buttons, enter windows, select text, bring up menus, and scroll in windows. If you are the first on your block to use a bit-mapped display with a mouse, you can use the system from the hints we give you here, or look in the User's Guide.* We will give you a very careful step-by-step explanation of how to navigate and enter programs. At the back of this book you will find a user interface pocket reference card. *Pull it out and use it as a reminder.*

To start Smalltalk you probably have to do something sophisticated like typing @ST80. If the incantation at your site is different, write it here:

If that doesn't work, ask a friend or use the on-line help facility of the operating system from which you are trying to launch Smalltalk. The display should now look similar to the figure below. It may differ if some windows are closed, collapsed, or not there at all (see Figure 2.1).

We would like to say that there is just one standard way to drive a Smalltalk-80 system, and that this book teaches it. Unfortunately, there are two ways that your system might be different from the standard version, depending on the numbers of mouse buttons** and the

---

* As mentioned in the preface, "User's Guide" refers to *Smalltalk-80: The Interactive Programming Environment*, by Adele Goldberg. In the User's Guide, read Sections 1.1 for the mouse, 2.5 for entering windows, 3.1 for selecting text, and 2.3 for scrolling.

** *How many buttons are there on your mouse or pointing device?* If there are three buttons, then the descriptions we will give are correct, and you can skip to the second part of this footnote. We describe the three buttons as left, middle, and right. If your mouse has only one

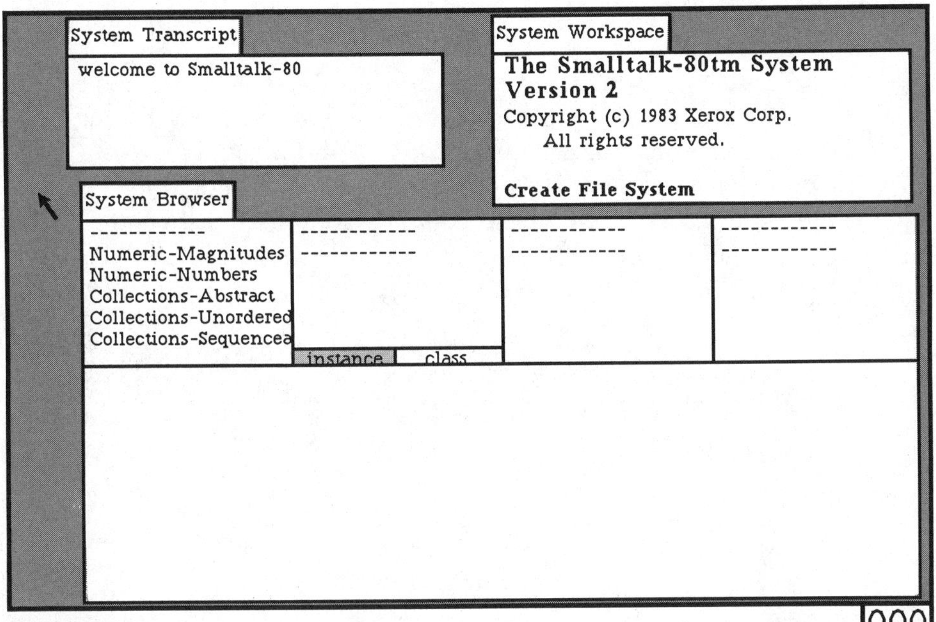

```
┌─────────────────────────────────┬──────────────────────────────────┐
│ System Transcript               │ System Workspace                 │
│ ┌─────────────────────────────┐ │ The Smalltalk-80tm System        │
│ │ welcome to Smalltalk-80     │ │ Version 2                        │
│ │                             │ │ Copyright (c) 1983 Xerox Corp.   │
│ │                             │ │    All rights reserved.          │
│ └─────────────────────────────┘ │                                  │
│ ┌─────────────────────────┐     │ Create File System               │
│ │ System Browser          │     │                                  │
│ │ -----------  ----------- │ ----------- │ ----------- │
│ │ Numeric-Magnitudes ----------- │ ----------- │ ----------- │
│ │ Numeric-Numbers         │     │                                  │
│ │ Collections-Abstract    │     │                                  │
│ │ Collections-Unordered   │     │                                  │
│ │ Collections-Sequenced   │     │                                  │
│ │       instance   class  │     │                                  │
└─────────────────────────────────┴──────────────────────────────────┘
```

Figure 2.1

version of the Smalltalk system***. We call the three mouse buttons "left," "middle," and "right." In some Smalltalk methods, and in the other Smalltalk books, the buttons are called, respectively, "red,"

---

button, you will need to do something different when we say "click the middle button." Apple computers use position on the screen in conjunction with their single mouse button to provide three virtual buttons for Smalltalk.

To use the "left button," point at anything "inside" the main part of a window and press the single mouse button.

To use the "middle button," move the cursor into the bar at the left edge of the window. When the cursor changes into a picture of a menu ▦ , press the mouse button. (The cursor can change into four different shapes inside the bar, depending on its horizontal position.)

To use the "right button," move the cursor into the title tab at the top of the window and press the mouse button.

Alternatively, if you don't like that way of indicating middle and right buttons, there is another way to do it on Apple machines. Instead of using the position of the cursor to encode the buttons, you can use the "Enter" and "Option" keys as you would use shift keys.

To get the "middle button," press the mouse button while you are holding down the "Option" key.

To get the "right button," press the mouse button while you are holding down the "Enter" key.

*** *Is your Smalltalk-80 system a License 1 system or a License 2 system?* Unless you are using a Macintosh, the answer is probably "License 2" (see the table in the preface to see which license you have). The Smalltalk books by Goldberg and Robson describe the License 2 system, and this book also uses the License 2 conventions. The main difference is the choice of items the user has in the middle-button menu in the browser. If you have License 2, just follow the description in the text. Where possible we will note the License 1 deviations in footnotes or parentheses. Macintosh users may find this slightly inconvenient, but bear with us. (Besides Apple, Digital Equipment and Hewlett-Packard also have the option to sell Smalltalk-80 systems under License 1.)

"yellow," and "blue." These kinds of mix-ups may seem childish, but we are here to explore a young subject.

We start by dealing with the display. The largest window on the screen is labeled **System Browser**. It is used for browsing through the many snippets of program that make up the Smalltalk system. The browser shows pieces of code according to a classification scheme, and is the main place where code is composed and edited. Looking at the browser, you see menus in four areas across the top. These areas are labeled A, B, C, and D in Figure 2.2. Area E is the "text" section

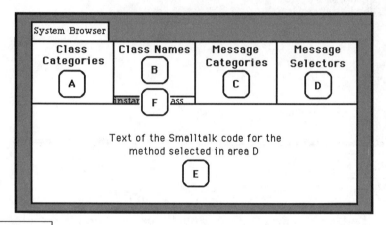

Figure 2.2

where you will edit programs. The broadest categories are in the left menu; after you have chosen one of these categories, a more specific menu appears to its right. You will work from left to right across the four menus, and then see or create a piece of program in the bottom window. For now, don't worry about the significance or meaning of the four menus in the browser.

With traditional programming systems one creates a new program that is loosely linked to other programs via the operating system. In Smalltalk, on the other hand, every program is just a piece of the whole system, and the pieces are linked together. This Zen-like approach to programming means we must find a place for Tower of Hanoi before we can write the program. Let's create a **games** section in one of the more generic parts of the system.

To place the **games** category in the Smalltalk hierarchy:

(1) "Enter the window" of the browser. Do this by moving the cursor inside the browser. One of the windows on your screen is actively listening to your mouse and keyboard. If the label that says **System Browser** is shown in reverse video (white let-

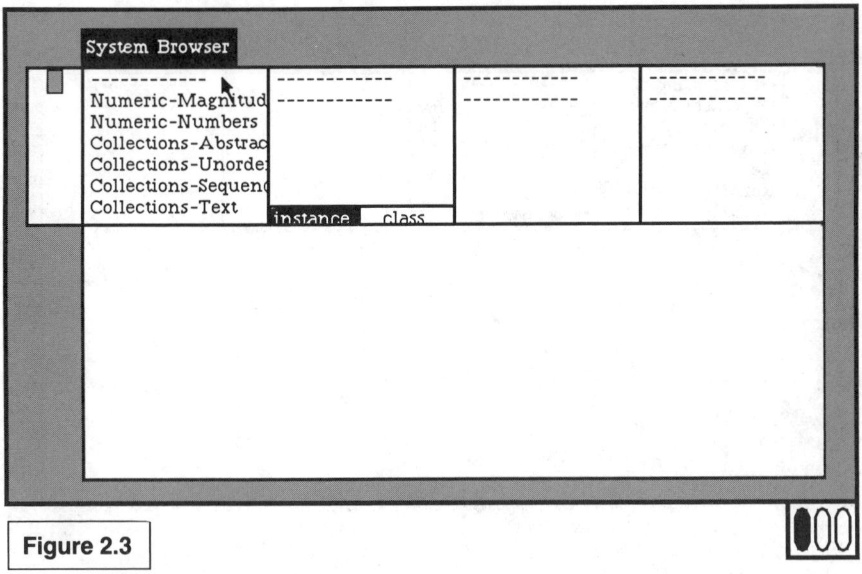

Figure 2.3

ters on a black background), then the browser is the active
window. If the browser is not already active, briefly press and
release the left mouse button.* This action is called a "click."
The System Browser should look like Figure 2.3.

(2) Move the cursor into area A of the browser. Look for **Kernel-
Objects**, one of the categories in area A. It is not in the visible
portion of area A, so you will have to move the menu to find
it. We call this "scrolling." Just move the cursor into the vertical rectangle at the left edge of the window. You will notice
the cursor changing shape as you move the mouse from side
to side. (If the scroll bar suddenly disappears, move the cursor back into area A.) The horizontal position of the cursor
determines which cursor is showing. Move to the right side
of the scroll bar until the cursor shows an upward-pointing
arrow. When you click, the line beside the cursor will go to
the top of the window (see Figure 2.4).

To move the menu down, move the cursor to the left
edge of the bar and get the down-pointing arrow. A click now
will send the line at the top of the window to where the cursor
is (the farther down the cursor is, the more text will scroll
down). Try it a few times. You are looking for **Kernel-Objects**.
It is near the middle of the list, between the **Graphics-** items

---

* If you are using a Macintosh 512K system, you are running Apple's "Level 0" Smalltalk-80
system. The browser window may not be on the screen. Instead it is "collapsed" and shows as
just a label. If so, put the cursor in the label, press and hold the mouse button, and a pop-up
menu will appear. Move the cursor to **frame** and let up on the button. The browser will expand
into a window, and you can do Step 1 above.

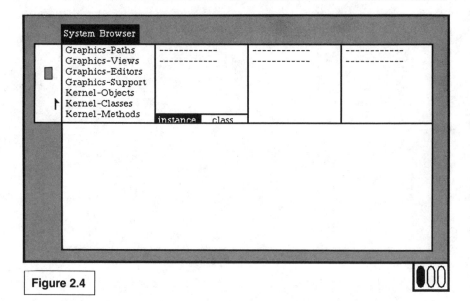

Figure 2.4

and the **Interface-** items (License 1 users will find it after the **Interface-** items). The Smalltalk system allows you to scroll almost any window (see Figure 2.5). If you want to know more about scrolling, see Section 2.3 of the User's Guide.

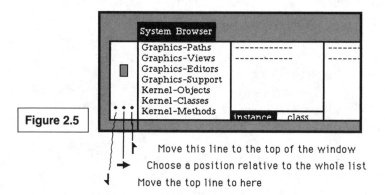

Figure 2.5

(3) Select **Kernel-Objects**. When we say "select" an item we mean place the cursor over the item and click the left mouse button. (Remember? Briefly press and release. The pocket reference card at the back of this book summarizes the various ways the mouse can be used to select an item or move around in the browser. Pull out the card and use it as you read.) In Figure 2.6, the three ovals at the bottom right of the figures represent the left, middle, and right mouse buttons. Any oval that is black means that that button is being pressed. The figure shows the screen as it is before the blackened button is

System Browser

Graphics-Paths
Graphics-Views
Graphics-Editors
Graphics-Support
Kernel-Objects
Kernel-Classes
Kernel-Methods

instance   class

Figure 2.6

released. A new menu will appear in area B after you click on **Kernel-Objects**.

(4) Move to area B and select Object (see Figure 2.7).

(5) In area F, make sure the word **instance** is selected (shown in reverse video). If it is not, click it once. (In this book we will never use the **class** setting, so be sure that **instance** stays selected.)

(6) Now let's add a category in which to put new procedures. Move to area C. Press and hold down the middle mouse but-

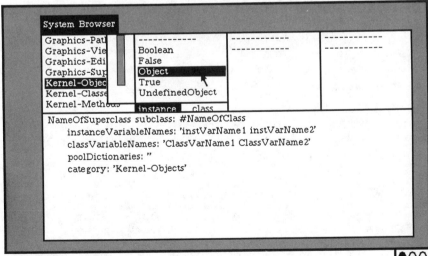

System Browser

Graphics-Pat
Graphics-Vie
Graphics-Edi
Graphics-Sup
Kernel-Objec
Kernel-Classe
Kernel-Meth

Boolean
False
Object
True
UndefinedObject

instance   class

NameOfSuperclass subclass: #NameOfClass
    instanceVariableNames: 'instVarName1 instVarName2'
    classVariableNames: 'ClassVarName1 ClassVarName2'
    poolDictionaries: ''
    category: 'Kernel-Objects'

Figure 2.7

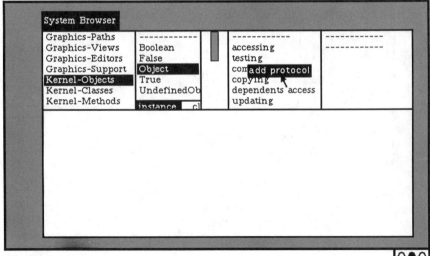

Figure 2.8

ton. (Macintosh users hold down "Option" while pressing the mouse button.) A menu will pop up onto the screen. For obscure technical reasons, this kind of menu is known as a "pop-up menu." This menu has only one item, **add protocol**.* Make sure the cursor is on **add protocol** (it shows in reverse video) and gently release the button to choose the item (see Figure 2.8).

A little window will appear, asking you to type a name. There will be an old name there in reverse video, so just type the word *games* and press the return key (see Figure 2.9). The window will disappear. If nothing happened when you typed, make sure the cursor is inside the little window.

(7) The name of our new section, **games**, will appear and be selected for us in area C. Move the cursor into area E at the bottom of the browser (see Figure 2.10).

You are about to type in the Smalltalk version of the Tower of Hanoi. But first you need to learn about the Smalltalk text editor. Most editors have modes. This means that if you are editing text and you stop to answer the phone, when you return you will have to remember

---

* If your menu does not have the item **add protocol** on it, you have a License 1 system and must do a little more work. Do not choose any items from the menu (move out of the menu and release the button). Move into area B and hold down the middle button. (Hold down "Option" and the mouse button.) Move to the item called **protocols** and release the mouse button. After a moment, a long list will appear in area E. Move the cursor there, and without clicking anywhere, type ('games') and press return. Be sure the parentheses and single quotes are there. Keep the cursor in area E, and choose **accept** from the middle-button menu (use the "Option" key). Now go on to Step 7.

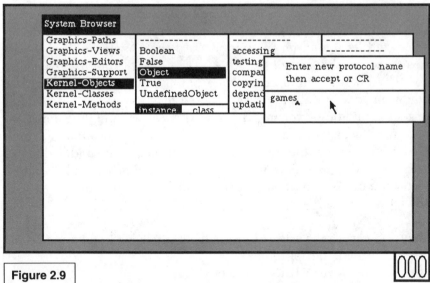

Figure 2.9

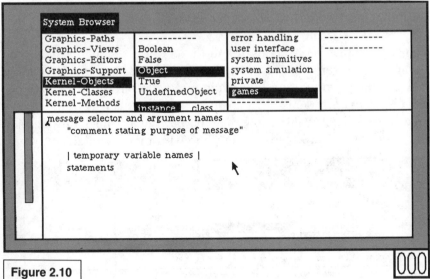

Figure 2.10

what mode you were in (insertion, deletion, or searching) before you
can continue. Smalltalk uses a "modeless" editor, meaning that there
is nothing to remember. There are fewer commands than in a modal
editor, and any of these actions may be performed at any time.

You modify text by clicking somewhere in the text and then typing; what you type goes where you clicked. When you click in the text,
a little mark, like this ▲, appears to tell you where the new text will be
inserted.

You select existing text by pointing in front of the first character, holding down the left button, moving the cursor to after the last character, and letting up on the button. Text that is selected is shown in reverse video. As you can see, this text is selected, but this text is not.

The middle button gives you a pop-up menu with the standard editor functions (Macintosh users should hold down the "Option" key to get the middle-button menu). You only need a few of these functions now (a full list appears in Appendix 1). To pick one, just hold the middle button, point at the item you want, and release the middle button. This is called "choosing" a menu item. If you are in the middle-button menu and decide not to take any of the choices, move out of the menu and let up on the button.

copy   Copies the selected text without removing it (the copy is held in a buffer off the screen).

cut   Removes what you selected.

paste   Replaces the current selection with the last thing you cut, copied, or typed. If nothing is selected to be replaced, it inserts the text where the little mark is.

You replace text by selecting it and then typing. As soon as you type the first character, the old text is cut out. If you have trouble editing and no one is around to ask, consult Section 3.3 in the User's Guide. Before going on, practice by making a bunch of changes in the text in area E (see Figure 2.11). Now that you have had a quick introduction to the editor, we are ready to continue with the example.

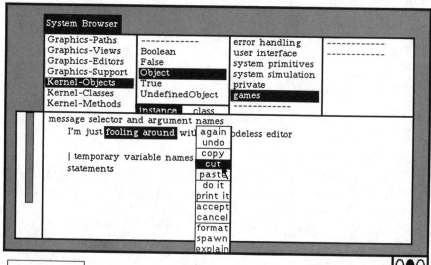

Figure 2.11

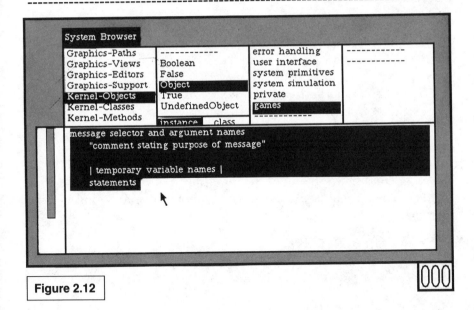

Figure 2.12

(8) In area E, select all the text: Move the cursor to just before the first character and press and hold the left mouse button. Still holding the button, move the mouse down below all the text. Release the button. All the text should be selected; if not, click once somewhere in area E and try again (see Figure 2.12).

(9) What you are about to type will replace the selected text. (You may want to use the tab key to get the proper indentation.) Type the program shown here:

```
moveTower: height from: fromPin to: toPin using: usingPin
    "Recursive procedure to move the disk at a height from one
    pin to another pin using a third pin"
    (height > 0) ifTrue: [
        self moveTower: (height − 1) from: fromPin to: usingPin using: toPin.
        self moveDisk: fromPin to: toPin.
        self moveTower: (height − 1) from: usingPin to: toPin using: fromPin]

    "This comment gives an example of how to run this program.
    Select the following and choose 'do it' from the middle-button menu.
        (Object new) moveTower: 3 from: 1 to: 3 using: 2"
```

(10) Read over what you have typed. Including the comments, there should be 19 colons, 4 periods, and 4 double quote marks, and possibly some words as well. Do the parentheses and brackets match? Is everything spelled right? Also, remember that capital letters are used as visual separators, so be sure that you have typed the program in exactly as it appears above. To correct something, select the incorrect characters (press on the left button before the first character and let up after the last character), then type the right characters.

(11) Hold down the middle button, move to the **accept** item, and release (that is, "choose" **accept** from the middle-button pop-up menu). See Figure 2.13.

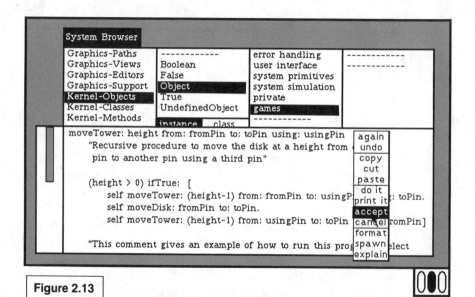

Figure 2.13

This attempts to compile, link, and load what we have just typed. **accept** reads everything in area E, so you don't need to select any text. However, the system will ask you a question before it absorbs what you typed (see Figure 2.14).

(12) This question will appear as a new kind of menu on the screen. When the compiler finds a syntax error, an undefined variable, or a new procedure name, it puts up this menu. Look at what the menu says across the top. It should say, "moveDisk:to: is a new message" because you have not yet defined that method. The system does not recognize the method name and wants to know if you made a typo or are

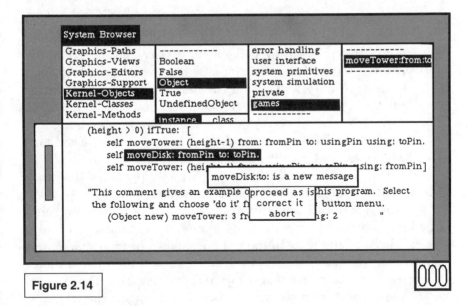

Figure 2.14

just mentioning a new procedure. Reassure the system by clicking **proceed as is**. (In License 1 systems, the menu says **Unknown selector...** across the top. Click on the first item in the menu, which should be moveDisk:to:.) If the menu says something else across the top, or if a little note is inserted into the text, then you've probably made an error typing in this method. To get help in locating the problem, read the section on troubleshooting at the end of this chapter.

When the system successfully accepts our new procedure, it will list the name of the procedure in area D, and show the name in bold-face in area E. Don't try to run the program yet; the code you wrote calls another procedure named moveDisk:to: and we haven't typed that in yet. (If you try, the system will say it doesn't understand moveDisk: to:.) In the next chapter we will define that method, and run our program.

Congratulations. You have just grafted a new procedure into your Smalltalk-80 system.

TROUBLESHOOTING WHEN YOU accept A METHOD

Let's review what can happen when you ask the system to **accept** a method (procedure) you just typed. If you have any trouble in later chapters, you can refer to this section to help you find the problem. If this section becomes tedious, just skip it and go on to Chapter 3.

• If the method contains any message selector (procedure name) that has not been mentioned before, Smalltalk will put a menu on the screen. When we defined moveTower:from:to:using: in the previous section, the selector moveDisk:to: had never been defined or used. The system put up a menu with the title **move-Disk:to: is a new message** (the menu is shown in Figure 2.14, in the previous section). Since it was indeed a new message, and since it was spelled the way we wanted it, we clicked **proceed as is**, and Smalltalk finished compiling the method. (In License 1 from Apple the menu would appear as **Unknown selector, please confirm, correct, or abort:**.)

• If the menu says something else across the top, you probably have a typo. The questionable phrase is mentioned and is also selected in the text. In the example shown in Figure 2.15, the phrase "to: usingPin" has been left out, and the system didn't recognize the rest of that name. If something like this happens, choose **abort** from the menu (click on it), correct the text, and choose **accept** again from the middle-button menu.

The *(method name)* **is a new message** menu is symptomatic of several different problems. Besides pinpointing a truly new message, or a piece missing from an old message, it may indicate that a period is missing at the end of a statement. If you mean to type:

```
self moveTower: (height − 1) from: fromPin to: usingPin using: toPin.
self moveDisk: fromPin to: toPin.
```

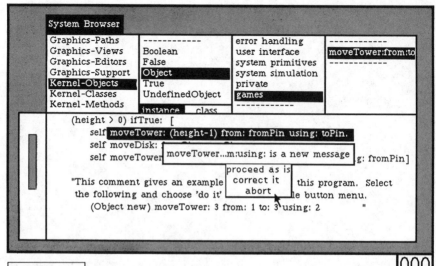

Figure 2.15

but forget the period separating the statements, the compiler will think that the whole thing is one giant message and will ask you about the new message moveTower:from:to:using:move-Disk:to:. If you spell a message name incorrectly, or fail to capitalize the right letters in a message name, the same kind of menu will appear.

- If the compiler detects a variable that has never been mentioned before, it puts up a menu that says **declare** *(variable name)* **as**. (In License 1 systems from Apple, the menu is titled **Unknown variable:** *(variable name)* **please correct, or abort:**.) In the menu are the choices for the type of the new variable. If the variable name is simply spelled wrong, you can invoke the spelling corrector by choosing **correct it** (or, if it shows in the menu, you can choose the correct spelling).
- There is another class of errors which is particularly hard to diagnose. If you type the method in area E of the browser, but previously forgot to choose the right settings in the other areas of the browser, strange things will happen. You will look at your code in area E, and see that it is typed perfectly, but the system will still refuse to **accept** it. If you have failed to select an item in areas C, B, or A, the browser will do one of three things when you choose **accept**. Area E may flash once, the message Nothing more expected: – > may be inserted at the start of the first line, or the system may ignore the **accept** command entirely. If you discover that nothing is selected in area C, select all the text you typed and choose **copy** from the middle-button menu. Then go to areas A, B, and C of the browser, choose the correct settings for this method, and **paste** your method into area E.
- In later chapters we will define several different classes of objects and define methods in each. If you have selected one class in area B (and something in area C), and if you try to **accept** a method that does not belong in this class, you will keep getting menus that ask you to declare variables. The compiler won't recognize the variables that belong to another class. When you realize that the method you typed really belongs in another class, **copy** it from area E, choose the correct class and category in areas B and C, and **paste** your method into the new area E.
- When the compiler detects a syntax error other than an unknown variable or message name, it inserts a little note into the text such as Argument expected: – >. If this happens, look at the text just after the note and try to find the problem. When you know what needs fixing, **cut** the little note from the text, make the

correction, and choose **accept** again. Error messages like this, which are inserted into the method and highlighted, are simple syntax errors. You will see them when you have unmatched single quotes, double quotes, brackets, or parentheses, or when a message that takes an argument is not followed by one.

For more details on errors that are detected when you choose **accept**, see Chapters 16 and 17 of the User's Guide.

RUNNING THE EXAMPLE

CONTINUING THE FIRST EXAMPLE

One must learn by doing the thing;
For though you think you know it,
You have no certainty until you try.

SOPHOCLES, *Trachiniae*

The Smalltalk programming environment tries to provide every tool you want for finding, viewing, writing, and running Smalltalk methods. The system can tell that a particular piece of text is a method by the window in which it is typed. Thus there is no need for special punctuation marking the beginning or end of a Smalltalk method. Every time you deal with a whole method, it is inside a window that expects a method, such as area E of the browser.

The method moveDisk:to: includes a couple of new things.

```
moveDisk: fromPin to: toPin
    "Move a disk from a pin to another pin. Print the results in the
      transcript window"
    Transcript cr.
    Transcript show: (fromPin printString, ' -> ', toPin printString).
```

The System Transcript is a window on the screen. It behaves like a traditional character-oriented terminal. The object that represents the transcript is held in the global variable, Transcript. The message cr tells the transcipt to append a carriage return. The message show: takes a string as an argument and appends it to the transcript. It also redisplays the text in the transcript window, so you can see it.

Each comma in the expression (fromPin printString, ' − > ', toPin printString) is not a piece of punctuation, but an operator like +. The operator (selector) comma means "concatenate two strings." In this case, fromPin printString returns a string, and the comma concatenates the literal string ' − > ' onto the end of it. The result of toPin printString is then concatenated to the end of that. When we work with arrays in a later chapter, you will see that an array also understands the message comma. It returns a new array consisting of itself concatenated with the argument.

RUNNING A PROGRAM

If you remember from our last episode, we defined a new method (procedure) whose selector (name) is moveTower:from:to:using:. Now we will type in moveDisk:to: and run the program.

We need to clear a space in the browser, in which to put our new method. Go to area D and find moveTower:from:to:using:. It is probably selected (reverse video). See Figure 3.1.

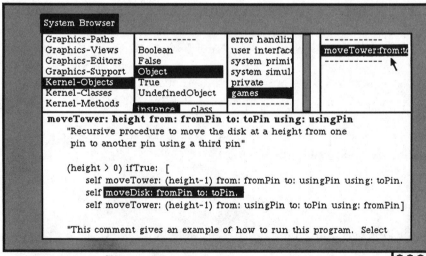

Figure 3.1

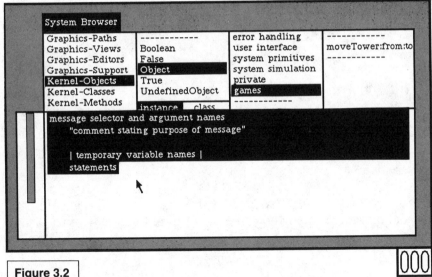

Figure 3.2

We don't want any method to be selected, so click once on moveTower:from:to:using: to "deselect" it. Now select all the text in area E (use the left button; press down at the beginning of the text, move to the end and release). See Figure 3.2.

Type in the code for moveDisk:to:

```
moveDisk: fromPin to: toPin
    "Move a disk from a pin to another pin. Print the results in the
     transcript window"
    Transcript cr.
    Transcript show: (fromPin printString, ' −> ', toPin printString).
```

Once again choose **accept** by holding down the middle button, moving to **accept**, and releasing. (We call this "accepting a method.") The procedure name (message selector) moveDisk:to: should appear in area D of the browser. If anything else happens, such as an error correction window appearing on the screen, consult the section on "Troubleshooting When You **accept** a Method" in Chapter 2.

Let's try the Tower of Hanoi using three disks. Move the cursor to the window labeled **System Transcript** (probably in the upper left corner of the display) and click the left button ("enter the window") (see Figure 3.3).

When the window wakes up, point to the end of the text, click once, and type:

```
(Object new) moveTower: 3 from: 1
to: 3 using: 2
```

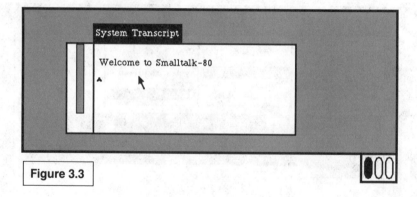

Figure 3.3

Select both lines of text and choose **do it** from the middle-button pop-up menu (see Figure 3.4).

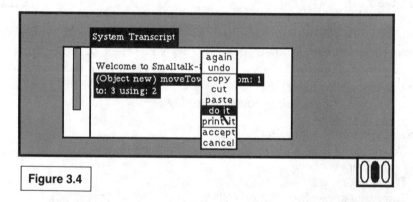

Figure 3.4

do it, as you might expect, tells Smalltalk to execute what you have selected. The System Transcript shows program output, just as a traditional character-oriented terminal does in other programming systems. This sequence of moves should scroll by:

```
1 -> 3
1 -> 2
3 -> 2
1 -> 3
2 -> 1
2 -> 3
1 -> 3
```

If you missed what was printed, you can scroll the transcript back to see lines above the window. Just move the cursor to the left edge of the scroll bar until the cursor shows a down-pointing arrow. When you

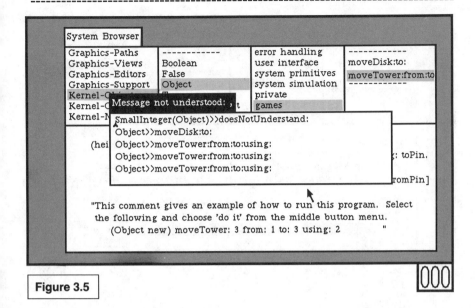

Figure 3.5

click, the line at the top of the window will come to where the cursor is.

If all goes well, you will see the numbers in the transcript. If not, an error window like the one in Figure 3.5 probably appeared on the screen.

If the error window appears, please read the troubleshooting section that appears after this section.

Let's run the program again with different arguments. Rather than typing the line over again, use a comment you typed earlier. Enter the browser (click once after moving to it) and click on **move-Tower:from:to:using:** in area D. At the bottom of the code, inside a comment, is an example of how to run the program. We can run it again with another height just by editing the comment to make the first argument (the height) be 4 instead of 3. Then select the example and say **do it** with the middle button. (Well, as most Smalltalk systems don't recognize human speech, you may have to use your fingers.) See Figure 3.6.

Smalltalk programmers traditionally show an example of how to use a given method in a comment inside that method. This means the scrap of code to run an example of the method is written only once, thereby avoiding the keystrokes of those long compound procedure names.

Before we go any further, please accept our congratulations! You have now written your first Smalltalk program. You could stop now and begin waxing eloquently about the strengths and weaknesses of

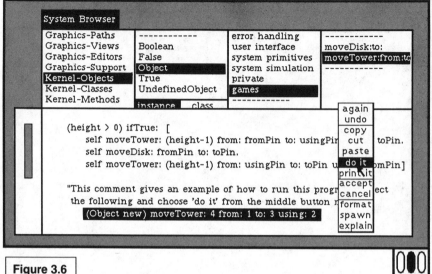

Figure 3.6

Smalltalk, but if you hang on a bit longer we promise there is more fun. After all, we haven't yet told you how to declare new data types.

Notice that we never declared the type of the arguments to our procedure, moveTower:from:to:using:. In this instance, Smalltalk is much more like LISP than Pascal, because Smalltalk variables can be any type. Without making changes to the procedures, we can actually run the program with strings as the names of the poles instead of integers! Furthermore, the height can be a floating point number. Try the example again with new pole names:

(Object new) moveTower: 3.0 from: 'North'
to: 'South' using: 'Telephone'

When you select this and choose **do it**, the transcript will show:

'North' −> 'South'
'North' −> 'Telephone'
'South' −> 'Telephone'
'North' −> 'South'
'Telephone' −> 'North'
'Telephone' −> 'South'
'North' −> 'South'

Smalltalk allows the same program to work on many different types of objects as long as they understand the same messages (operators and procedure names). For example, height need only understand > and −, and the pole numbers must only understand printString. Since every object understands printString, the method moveTower:from:to:using: is not very selective about its arguments.

TROUBLESHOOTING RUNTIME ERRORS

Let's review what to do if an error window appears on the screen while you are running your program. If you have any trouble in later chapters, you can refer to this section to help you find the problem. If this section becomes tedious, just skip it and go on to the next example.

Figure 3.5 in the section above shows a typical error window. The title tells you what happened. In this case it says, **Message not understood:** ,. The object that received the message comma did not know what to do in response to that message. Typically, this means that the receiving object is not the object you expected it to be when you wrote the code. The list inside the window shows the stack of nested procedure calls at the time of the error. It tells what methods were running or were waiting for an answer from methods they themselves called. In this example, the nesting is:

```
SmallInteger(Object)>>doesNotUnderstand:
Object>>moveDisk:to:
Object>>moveTower:from:to:using:
Object>>moveTower:from:to:using:
Object>>moveTower:from:to:using:
```

The title and the top line tell us that a SmallInteger did not understand the message comma. The integer was sent the message comma in the method for moveDisk:to: in class Object. This is the code we just wrote, so it is a prime suspect for errors. Close the error window by placing the cursor in the window and choosing **close** from the right-button pop-up menu. Enter the browser and look carefully at the code for moveDisk:to:, especially where the message comma is sent. (In this hypothetical example, the user left out one of the printString messages in the last line of moveDisk:to:.)

For the example programs in this book, the errors will come from code that you typed in. Concentrate your search on the code you entered and are trying for the first time. Later, when you are modifying programs on your own and get an error, you can open the error window by choosing **debug** from the middle-button menu. The window expands into a complete debugger, which is explained in detail in Chapters 18 and 19 of the User's Guide.

THE SECOND SMALLTALK EXAMPLE

----

*If a program is useful,
it will have to be changed.*
ANONYMOUS, *SIGPLAN Notices Vol. 2, No. 2*

So far we have called procedures and demonstrated output. Next we will modify our program to allow the user to type in the number of disks. Then we will learn how to save the program to a file on the disk. The method hanoi below asks the user for the number of disks and then calls moveTower:from:to:using:.

```
hanoi
    "Tower of Hanoi program. Asks user for height of stack of disks"

    | height aString |
    aString ← FillInTheBlank request: 'Please type the number of
disks in the tower, and <cr>'.
    height ← aString asNumber.
    Transcript cr.
    Transcript show: ('Tower of Hanoi for: ', height printString).
    self moveTower: height from: 1 to: 3 using: 2.

    "   (Object new) hanoi.   "
```

The third line of the method declares two local variables, height and aString. Although you do not need to declare the type of variables in Smalltalk, you do declare the names. Names enclosed in vertical bars at the beginning of a method are local to that method.

The next statement puts a fill-in-the-blank window on the screen and stores what the user typed into aString. Strings respond to the message **asNumber** which converts a string of digits (0–9) to a number. The result is stored in height. From there, we send a carriage return to the transcript, write some text there, and start the game running.

Left-arrow is the assignment operator; you can pronounce it as "gets." In one of the lines above, height gets aString asNumber.

When you are exploring the Smalltalk system, you will often be reading code. Reading code is easy if you can do two things: identify the objects, and understand the order in which messages are sent. All words that begin with a letter and don't end with a colon are objects, except those that immediately follow another object. In the expression aString asNumber, aString is an object and asNumber is a message.

Numbers, literal strings ('ABC'), literal characters ($A), and the results of all message sends are also objects. In a series of words without colons such as height printString size, the first word is an object, and the rest are message names. In (height printString) size, the token size is still a message name, since the expression in parentheses evaluates to an object. See if you can underline all the objects in the method hanoi. (Look again at the example in Chapter 2.)

The order in which messages are sent is a little more complicated. As you might expect, parentheses are used to show what to do first. We were amazed to find that parentheses are not required in any of the first three methods we wrote. We will have to concoct an example in which they are required. Let's combine two of the statements in hanoi into one.

height ← (FillInTheBlank request: 'Please type the number of disks in the tower, and <cr>') asNumber.

If the parentheses were not present, we would be sending the message asNumber to the literal string (the stuff in single quotes) instead of sending it to the result of the request: message. When you write code you can include as many parentheses as you want, but you may read code that has a minimum of parentheses, so it helps to know the order of evaluation.

Smalltalk has just two rules that tell which messages are sent before others. Messages without arguments (asNumber, cr, hanoi, etc.) are executed first. They take precedence over adjacent messages that are operators ($+$, $-$, *, $=$, $>$, comma, etc.). Thus aString size > 0 is the same as (aString size) > 0 and means send the message size to aString first. Operator messages are executed before adjacent messages whose names contain colons. Thus

Transcript show: ('Tower of Hanoi for ', height printString).

does not need parentheses to concatenate the two strings ('Tower of Hanoi for ' and the result of height printString) before they are sent as the argument of the show: message. This is all explained in Section 5.2 of the User's Guide. In general, we have included more parentheses than are needed in order to make the code easier to read.

All spaces, tabs, and carriage returns in Smalltalk code are meaningless to the system. Packed methods compile just as well as beautiful, poetically indented ones. An exception is the separator that is needed between two names that are both alphabetic. aStringasNumber must have a space between aString and asNumber or it looks like a single name. Also, a period at the end of a statement must be followed by a separator to distinguish it from a decimal point. Keep in mind that, besides your machine, there is another computer that needs to understand your code. It is the human brain, and it greatly prefers nicely spaced and indented code.

INSTALLING THE hanoi METHOD

To clear area E of the browser, you first have to choose **cancel** from the middle-button pop-up menu (in area E). **cancel** means that we don't want to keep the changes we made to the arguments of moveTower:from:to:using: in the comment. You may have noticed that the middle and right buttons are only used for pop-up menus. The right-button menu holds commands that act on an entire window, and the middle-button menu commands are specific to the area of the window that the cursor is in. The left button never has a pop-up menu on it, and is reserved for pointing and clicking on fixed menus.

Now click on moveTower:from:to:using: in area D to deselect it. If you forgot to say **cancel** before choosing another method, a window will ask you if you want to discard the old changes. To confirm, move the cursor into the **yes** box and click the left button (see Figure 3.7).*

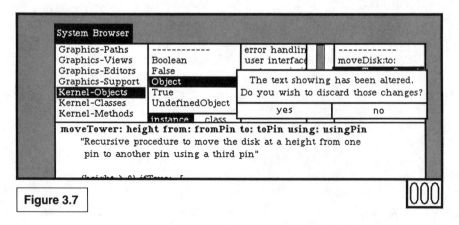

Figure 3.7

The browser should now look like it does in Figure 3.8. The text in area E is the default template for building a new method.

Select it all and replace it with the method below. The vertical bar character should be on your keyboard. If it is not, look for a broken vertical bar ¦. If your keyboard does not have a left-arrow key ←, use underscore _ instead. (Some keyboards have a ← key for moving the

---

* If you are running Apple's Level 0 Smalltalk system for the Macintosh 512K, your system may be missing two methods that hanoi uses. If so, please turn to Appendix 3, and follow the directions there to add the missing code to your system. All other readers may ignore Appendix 3.

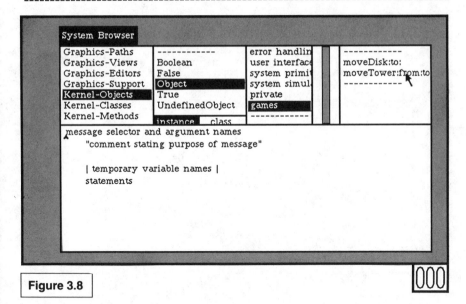

Figure 3.8

cursor. That key will probably not do the right thing. If the underscore key is the correct key to use on your system, Smalltalk will change it to a left arrow on the screen.)

```
hanoi
    "Tower of Hanoi program. Asks user for height of stack of disks"

    | height aString |
    aString ← FillInTheBlank request: 'Please type the number of
disks in the tower, and <cr>'.
    height ← aString asNumber.
    Transcript cr.
    Transcript show: 'Tower of Hanoi for: ', height printString.
    self moveTower: height from: 1 to: 3 using: 2.

    "   (Object new) hanoi.   "
```

Be sure to say **accept** (middle-button pop-up menu). If anything else happens, such as an error correction window appearing on the screen, consult the section on "Troubleshooting When You **accept** a Method" in Chapter 2.

We run this program by selecting the comment (Object new) hanoi (select inside the double-quote characters) and then choosing **do it** from the middle-button pop-up menu. A small window will appear and ask for the number of disks. Type any number and then hit the return key (see Figure 3.9).

It is interesting that few Smalltalk programmers use input param-

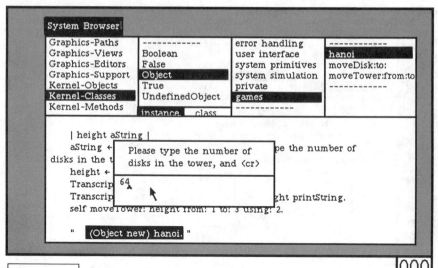

Figure 3.9

eters—they just edit a line that calls the program to include new values. Compiling and linking are so fast that there is rarely a reason to use input to get different values for parameters.

By the way, if you happened to type the number 64, and would like to change your mind to avoid bringing the universe to an end, just type *control C* (on a Macintosh it's *Command period*). To discard that semi-infinite process, close the error window (using the right–button pop-up menu to choose **close**) (see Figure 3.10). You can then make

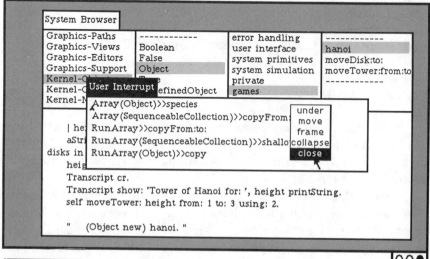

Figure 3.10

sure (Object new) hanoi is still selected, choose **do it**, and enter a less catastrophic number of disks.

Congratulations are called for again. You have now written a Smalltalk program that includes input as well as output.

SO YOU DON'T WANT TO TYPE THIS ALL IN AGAIN

*The first rule of intelligent tinkering
is to save all the parts.*

PAUL EHRLICH (environmentalist)

As with any interactive system, it is important to save your work. We would like to write out a file containing the three methods we have defined so far. Go into area C in the browser and hold down the middle button. Choose **file out** from the menu (see Figure 3.11). (If the menu says only **add protocol**, you need to move out of the menu, release the button, and select **games** again by clicking it with the left button.) The system will name the file Objects-games.st and write it on the disk.

If you are tired, this is a good time for a break. When you leave the Smalltalk system, you have two choices for saving your current state. If you want to start your next session exactly where you left off this time, you can "make a snapshot" and save the *entire* system on the disk. If you don't mind going back to the system from which you started this session, you can quit without saving anything. Since we just wrote out our program in a separate file, Objects-games.st, and we want to get experience bringing that file back into the system, let's quit without saving anything.

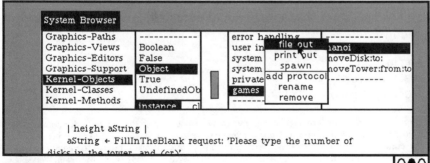

Figure 3.11

To exit Smalltalk, move the cursor into the gray background that is not in any window. Hold down the middle button, and choose **quit** from the menu. Another small menu will appear with three choices: **Save, then quit**; **Quit, without saving**; and **Continue**. Choose **Quit, without saving**. You will leave Smalltalk and enter your machine's operating system.

After getting back into Smalltalk, let's bring in the programs we wrote by reading the file we created. Move the cursor to the System Workspace window in the upper right corner of the screen.* We have not used this window before, but it contains many useful Smalltalk expressions that can be edited and executed. Enter the System Workspace window and scroll to the section called Files. (In License 1 systems the section is called Changes and Files.) You may need to get your sea legs again on the scroll bar. Side-to-side movement changes the cursor, and the up-arrow moves the line beside it to the top. Modify a line to say:

(FileStream oldFileNamed: 'Object-games.st') fileIn.

then select the whole line and choose **do it** from the middle-button menu (see Figure 3.12).

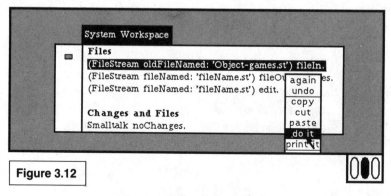

| **Figure 3.12** |

If all goes well, Smalltalk should put the following in the transcript window:

Filing in from:
Object-games.st
Object<games

---

* If no window on your screen is labeled System Workspace, move the cursor to the gray area and hold down the middle button. Choose **system workspace** from the menu that appears. When the cursor changes to a corner shape, press and hold the button and move the cursor to where you want the other corner of the new window. On the Mac 512K there is no System Workspace. Just type the line (FileStream oldFileNamed: 'Object-games.st') fileIn into the transcript, select it, and **do it**.

Now you can enter the browser, choose the category **Kernel-Objects**, choose Object, and see your methods waiting there for you.

The code in parentheses returns an object that is a stream on a file. The message fileIn causes the stream to invoke the compiler and to parse the contents of the file in a special way. The Smalltalk code in the file is in "Smalltalk-80 code file format." Not only are the methods you accepted there, but they are exactly where you put them in the browser. (Hackers who absolutely *must* know about code file format can read Glenn Krasner's article about it in Chapter 3 of *Smalltalk-80: Bits of History, Words of Advice.*)

┌─ ─ ─ ─ ─ ─ ─ ─ ─ ┐

4

└─ ─ ─ ─ ─ ─ ─ ─ ─ ┘

DEFINING A CLASS

THE CLASS TowerOfHanoi

If thought corrupts language,
language can also corrupt thought.
GEORGE ORWELL, *Nineteen Eighty-Four*

We bet several skeptical readers have doubts about whether this Tower of Hanoi algorithm really works. The disks are never identified or stored anywhere. The recursive calls leapfrog, one on top of another, and we really can't tell by looking at the code whether the algorithm works. If you were asked to print which disks were on which stacks after each move, you could not do it with the present data structures. We are now ready to use honest data structures and convince the skeptics.

We are going to make a data structure of three stacks and move the disks between them. Rather than have a separate variable for each stack, an array will hold the stacks so we can index them by pole number. The name of the variable for the array of stacks is **stacks**. We will use the characters A, B, C, etc., to represent the disks. What kind of variable should **stacks** be? In a conventional language, a local variable in the outer procedure would hold the towers. But Smalltalk uses a different, object-oriented style; it allows you to create a new kind of object to represent the Tower of Hanoi game—an object which contains variables to hold the stacks of disks.

In Smalltalk, you describe a new type of object before creating it. When you are done, the description works just as well for a whole class of objects. We call such an object description a "class." Any object created from the description is called an "instance" of the class. After we define a class of objects that holds the state of the Tower of Hanoi game, we have the power to create many examples, or instances, of the game with different numbers of disks and in different stages of progress through the game.

The definition of a class always begins by filling in a template.

```
Object subclass: #TowerOfHanoi
  instanceVariableNames: 'stacks '
  classVariableNames: ''
  poolDictionaries: ''
  category: 'Kernel-Objects'
```

In the next section we will see how to enter this definition into the system.

Every class in the Smalltalk system should have a comment associated with it. The comment is used to tell what the variables mean, and to explain what the class is for. The comment below for the class TowerOfHanoi is short, because we know you will have to type it later.

```
stacks is an Array of stacks.
    Each stack is an OrderedCollection.
    The objects we put on the stacks are characters.
    A is the smallest disk, B is larger, etc.
    addFirst: is the message for push, and removeFirst is pop.
```

For two of the three methods we have written, we are going to make a new version of the code inside class TowerOfHanoi. Here is the new version of hanoi.

```
hanoi
    "Tower of Hanoi program. Asks user for height of stack of disks"

    | height aString |
    aString ← FillInTheBlank request: 'Please type the number of
disks in the tower, and <cr>'.
    height ← aString asNumber.
    Transcript cr.
    Transcript show: 'Tower of Hanoi for:', height printString.
    stacks ← (Array new: 3) collect: [:each | OrderedCollection new].
    (height to: 1 by: −1) do: [:each | (stacks at: 1) addFirst:
        (Character value: ($A asciiValue) + each −1) ].
    self moveTower: height from: 1 to: 3 using: 2.

    "      (TowerOfHanoi new) hanoi.           "
```

This method serves to illustrate a few more features of the Smalltalk language. Let's walk through the code, commenting on the new language features as we find them. The first few lines are unchanged from before. hanoi has two local variables and asks the user for the number of disks. We want **stacks** to be a 3-element array, with each element of the array being a stack of disks. Since there are no type declarations in Smalltalk, we need to execute statements to create objects of the right type (instances of the right class). The statement assigning a value to **stacks** does this, and we will examine it in pieces. Smalltalk uses the **new:** method to create a new object. To make an array of 3 elements, you just say

Array new: 3

and you make a stack by saying

OrderedCollection new

(Smalltalk generally calls aggregate data types "collections"; and since the elements in a stack are ordered, a stack is considered an "ordered collection.")

We are going to skip the sixth line in the method hanoi, and consider the seventh and eighth lines. When we go back and explain the sixth, it will be easier to understand. The Smalltalk statement on the seventh and eighth lines is a "do loop." Besides iteration, it also includes array indexing, number conversion, and stack operations. We'll explain the pieces before we show you the whole thing. The standard Smalltalk iteration message is do:, and a fine example is

(1 to: height) do: [:each | *statements*].

This does exactly what you would expect, with **each** being the iteration variable whose value goes from 1 to **height** by increments of 1. The colon in :each means that a new value of **each** will be supplied each time the block is evaluated (as usual with iteration variables). The vertical bar acknowledges the fact that we are creating **each** as a local variable to the block (delimited by brackets). It can only be used within the block. A backwards counting loop would be

(height to: 1 by: − 1) do: [:each | *statements*].

How do you index arrays? The at: message selector (operator) is the answer, so you refer to the first element of **stacks** by stacks at: 1.

The remaining operations create characters that represent disks and then push them onto a stack. Using standard methods that are part of the Smalltalk system, you can convert an integer n to its corresponding ASCII character by

Character value: n.

The method to push an element onto a stack is addFirst:.

Now put it all together. Disk A should be the top disk, so push the last disk onto the stack last. From height to 1 by minus 1, make the corresponding character (. . . C, B, A) and push it onto the stack of tower number 1:

```
(height to: 1 by: − 1) do: [:each | (stacks at: 1) addFirst:
  (Character value: ($A asciiValue) + each − 1)].
```

The second line takes the ASCII value of the character A and adds the disk number minus 1. It then turns that back into a character to give the letters of the alphabet in order. $A is the literal character A.

Looking again at the sixth line of the hanoi method, where the stacks are created:

```
stacks ← (Array new: 3) collect: [:each | OrderedCollection new].
```

Smalltalk has several methods for transforming aggregate data types (collections); collect: is a popular example. The general form is

x collect: y.

This creates a new collection the same size as x, performing the operations specified in the block of code y to initialize each element. Let's make an array with 3 elements, with each element a new stack (OrderedCollection), and store the result in stacks:

```
stacks ← (Array new: 3) collect: [:each | OrderedCollection new].
```

Think of collect: as being just like do:. The local variable each is like an iteration variable, except that its values come from the collection (Array new: 3). Notice that after the value of each is assigned (on each iteration), we are totally ignoring it. The new values that we are collecting, a bunch of brand-new OrderedCollection's, can be constructed without reference to what was in the array before. (You may be curious what value each actually has. It is, in turn, each of the nils in the array we just created.) The message collect: is, in fact, a control structure that both creates a new collection and runs a loop to get its initial values.

As before, the last line of the hanoi method (before the comment) sends the method moveTower:from:to:using: to self.

Now let's look at the new method for moveDisk:to:.

```
moveDisk: fromPin to: toPin
    "Move a disk from a pin to another pin. Print the results in the
        transcript window"
    | disk |
    disk ← (stacks at: fromPin) removeFirst.
    (stacks at: toPin) addFirst: disk.
    Transcript cr.
    Transcript show: (fromPin printString, ' − > ', toPin printString, ' ').
    Transcript nextPut: disk.
    Transcript endEntry
```

The method pops a disk off the "from" stack into the local variable disk and pushes it onto the "to" stack. Then it prints the move along with the name of the disk that was moved. You already know how to index (at:) and push an element (addFirst:). You might guess that removeFirst pops the stack, so you pop from one and push to another by

```
    disk ← (stacks at: fromPin) removeFirst.
    (stacks at: toPin) addFirst: disk.
```

In the System Transcript window we print a carriage return, the "from" pole, the "to" pole, and append a space. The message nextPut: sends a single character (the disk's name) to the transcript. We must send endEntry afterwards to make the window refresh itself and show the character. (We didn't do this in the previous version because the method for show: has its own call on endEntry.)

HOW TO CREATE A NEW CLASS

Picking up our narrative, you'll remember we left you just after you heroically figured out how to save the universe by stopping the Tower of Hanoi with 64 disks. Now that the universe is assured of continuing, we can create a new class called TowerOfHanoi. In area A of the browser, make sure that the category **Kernel-Object** is selected.

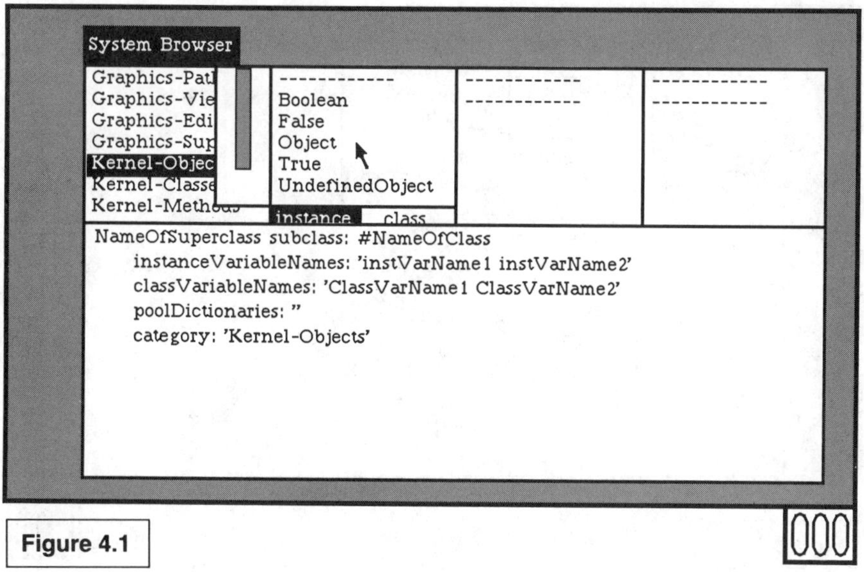

Figure 4.1

In area B, deselect the class **Object** (click on it) if it is currently selected (see Figure 4.1).

Replace the template in area E with the definition below. If you don't want to type the whole thing, you can edit the template in area E until it looks exactly like the definition below. The parts you need to change are underlined. (Be sure to **cut** out the stuff inside the single quotes at the end of the third line.) When you are checking the code you have typed against the code here, you may find it helpful to move the cursor along to keep your place on the screen.

Object subclass: #TowerOfHanoi
    instanceVariableNames: 'stacks'
    classVariableNames: ' '
    poolDictionaries: ''
    category: 'Kernel-Objects'

accept the definition (middle-button pop-up menu in area E). Sections 12.1 to 12.4 in the User's Guide have more details about class definitions. TowerOfHanoi should appear in the list in area B.

Now that you know about classes, the layout of the browser window should make more sense. Area A is a menu of categories of classes. Area B is a menu of individual classes within the category you have chosen. Area C is a menu of categories of methods (these are called "protocols") within the currently selected class. In area D, individual method names appear in the menu. In particular, moving across our

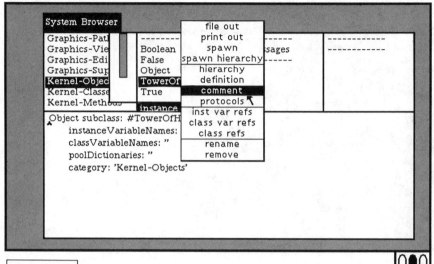

Figure 4.2

browser, we are in the category **Kernel-Objects** and are looking at the class TowerOfHanoi. We are going to define the message category **games** within the class and then install the method hanoi. The middle-button pop-up menu in each area has actions and requests that operate on the thing you have selected in that menu.

Every class should have a comment. In area B, choose **comment** from the middle-button menu (see Figure 4.2).

Now type the explanatory comment below. (License 1 users beware. You must type your comment inside the single quotes in area E. Do not erase the text that says TowerOfHanoi comment:. All normal License 2 users can simply replace the entire contents of area E with the text below.)

stacks is an Array of stacks.
    Each stack is an OrderedCollection.
    The objects we put on the stacks are characters.
    A is the smallest disk, B is larger, and so on.
    addFirst: is the message for push, and removeFirst is pop.

Say **accept**, move to area C (the message category menu), and add the category **the game**. We've added categories before; use the middle-button pop-up menu to choose **add protocol**, type *the game*, and press the return key. (If you are a License 1 user, you must go to area B and choose **protocols** from the middle-button menu. Type *('the game')* in area E and **accept**.) An entry for **the game** should appear in the message category menu, area C (License 1 users should enter area C and select it).

Now move the methods we already have into the new class you created. Rather than making you type them again, Smalltalk lets you use the text editor to move them from one place in the Smalltalk class structure to another. The easiest way to do this is to create a second browser that is dedicated to this new class and then use the **copy** and **paste** commands to move the methods from the old browser to the new one:

(1) To create a new browser, enter area B (the class names menu) and choose **spawn** from the middle-button pop-up menu (it's called **browse** in License 1 systems).

(2) Smalltalk will ask you where you want to place the new browser on the display. The question will be phrased as a corner cursor (see Figure 4.3). Imagine where you want your new browser

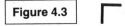

Figure 4.3

on the screen and what shape it should be. Try to pick an area that overlaps as little as possible the area of the old browser. Move the cursor to the best place for the upper left-hand corner of the new browser. Once there, hold the left button down and the cursor will change to a lower right corner cursor (see Figure 4.4).

Figure 4.4

While still holding the button, move the mouse to where you want the lower right hand corner of the browser. When you let up on the button you will see the new browser. This operation with the corner cursor is called "framing a window." You can reframe any Smalltalk window at any time by using the right-button menu and selecting **frame**.

(3) The new browser (Figure 4.5) looks different because it is for only one class, namely TowerOfHanoi. This browser is really the same as the old one, except that area A is gone, and the others are rearranged. Figure 4.6 identifies the areas of the new browser, which is called a Class Browser.

(4) Go back to the System Browser (the original browser). Wake it up by pointing in it and clicking. This brings it to the front of the display, onto the top of the stack of overlapping windows (see Figure 4.7).

(5) Select the class Object in area B (the class name menu) of the System Browser and the category **games** in area C (you may

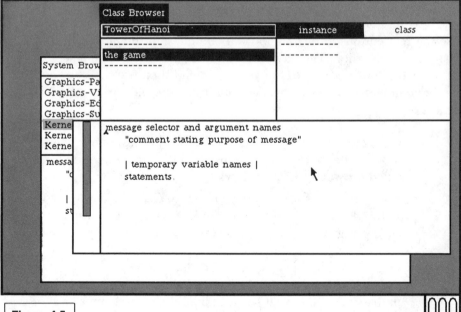

Figure 4.5

have to scroll to find it; use the upward-pointing arrow). Select hanoi in area D.

(6) Go down to the text area E of the System Browser and select all the text (reverse-video everything). (If you can't see the

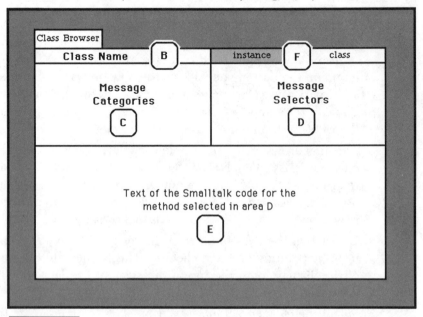

Figure 4.6

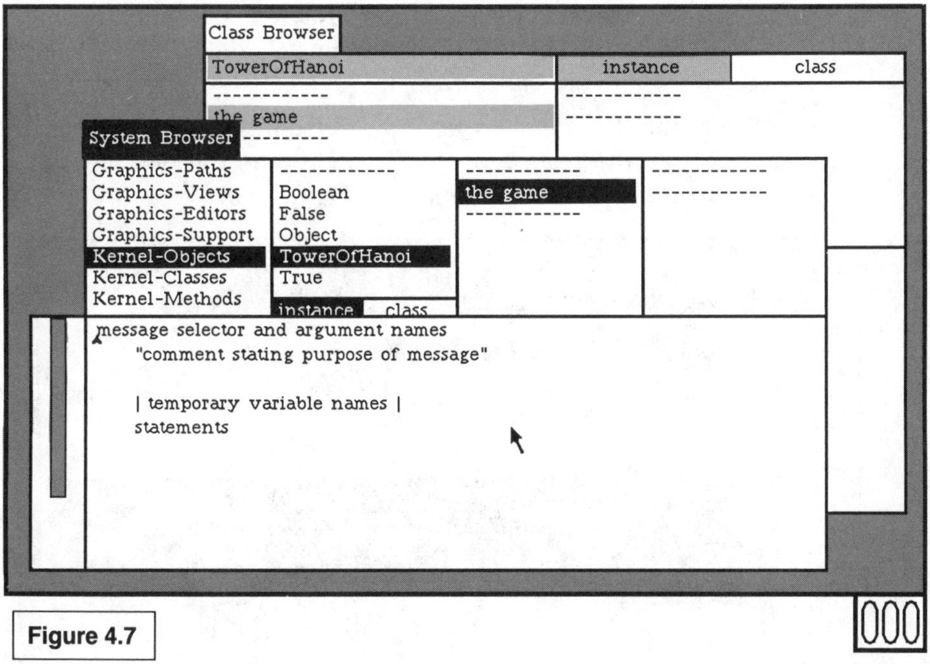

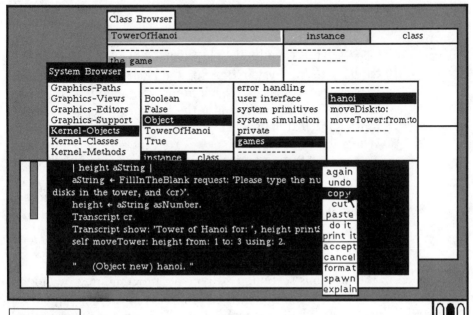

Figure 4.7

entire method at once in area E, you can still select it. Slowly
double-click the left button in front of the first character in
area E.) Use the middle-button pop-up menu and choose **copy**
to copy the method (see Figure 4.8).

Figure 4.8

(7) Go to the **Class Browser** (the new browser). Click in it to enter it (wake it up). The category **the game** should still be selected in area C (if not, select it).

(8) Go to the text area E, where the default method is displayed. Select all the text, and use the middle-button pop-up menu to **paste** the copied method (see Figure 4.9).

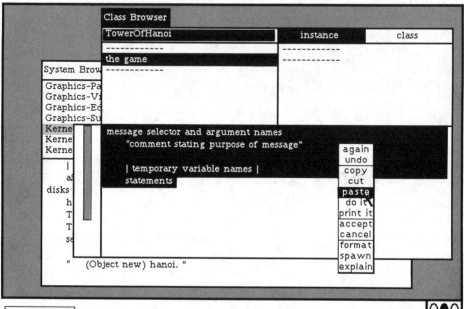

Figure 4.9

(9) **accept** the new method and its name will appear in area D.

(10) Go back to the **System Browser** and click to enter it. In area D, select moveDisk:to:. Using Steps 6 through 9 above, copy the moveDisk:to: method into the new browser. It is okay to replace the text of hanoi in area E, once it has been accepted. Whenever you accept the new text, if the message selector at its start is different from the old one, the browser will know you want to define a new method (don't copy the method moveTower:from:to:using:). As you are about to **accept** moveDisk:to: in area E of the new browser, the screen should look like Figure 4.10.

Now we are ready to make changes to these methods, as we discussed in the previous section. This type of "programming by modification" is common in Smalltalk. (Indeed; this is the way people do it in all languages; Smalltalk just makes it easy.) Select the hanoi method

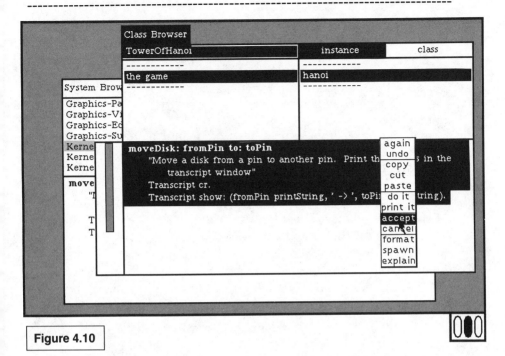

Figure 4.10

in the new browser in area D. Make the underlined changes shown below. (The pocket reference card or Appendix 1 has a refresher on text editing.) Check your changes and **accept** them.

hanoi
    "Tower of Hanoi program. Asks user for height of stack of disks"

    | height aString |
    aString ← FillInTheBlank request: 'Please type the number of
disks in the tower, and <cr>'.
    height ← aString asNumber.
    Transcript cr.
    Transcript show: 'Tower of Hanoi for: ', height printString.
    stacks ← (Array new: 3) collect: [:each | OrderedCollection new].
    (height to: 1 by: -1) do: [:each | (stacks at: 1) addFirst:
        (Character value: ($A asciiValue) + each -1)].
    self moveTower: height from: 1 to: 3 using: 2.

    "   (TowerOfHanoi new) hanoi.   "

    After accepting the changes, select moveDisk:to: in area D, make the underlined changes, and **accept** the revised method. If anything goes wrong with **accept**ing the revisions, consult the section on "Troubleshooting When You **accept** a Method" in Chapter 2.

```
moveDisk: fromPin to: toPin
    "Move a disk from a pin to another pin. Print the results in the
        transcript window"
    | disk |
    disk ← (stacks at: fromPin) removeFirst.
    (stacks at: toPin) addFirst: disk.
    Transcript cr.
    Transcript show: (fromPin printString, ' − > ', toPin printString, ' ').
    Transcript nextPut: disk.
    Transcript endEntry.
```

After checking, be sure to **accept**. Notice that you did not copy the method for moveTower:from:to:using: to your new class. This is because TowerOfHanoi is below class Object in the class hierarchy and the version of moveTower:from:to:using: in class Object will do everything we want. TowerOfHanoi inherits all methods from classes above it in the class hierarchy, so Smalltalk will find the existing version. You copied the other messages because we wanted to change them for use in TowerOfHanoi. We will cover inheritance in greater detail in the next chapter.

Run the program by executing:

(TowerOfHanoi new) hanoi.

(**select** it in the comment in the hanoi method and then choose **do it**.)

If the program is run with three disks, the System Transcript window should contain:

```
1 − > 3 A
1 − > 2 B
3 − > 2 A
1 − > 3 C
2 − > 1 A
2 − > 3 B
1 − > 3 A
```

If anything untoward happens (as it does so often in this young computer age), turn back to the section on "Troubleshooting Runtime Errors" on page 35 of Chapter 3.

Notice that you can still say (Object new) hanoi and get the same output as you got before we defined TowerOfHanoi. The method that is in control in both programs is moveTower:from:to:using:. Not only is it the same name; it is exactly the same code. How can the same main program get two different results? Different objects are sent the message moveTower:from:to:using: and thus inside that method self represents a different object. Object and TowerOfHanoi have separate definitions of moveDisk:to:, so when moveTower:from:to:using: sends the message, different code runs and the action is different.

The ability to have messages of the same name in two different classes, plus the fact that variables can be of any type, allows programmers reuse code and to avoid defining the same algorithm in several variations. Because Smalltalk acts differently when the same message is sent to different objects, all code contains an extra level of parameterization, allowing Smalltalk to share code extensively. The existence of only one copy of the code for each algorithm in the system is a major reason for Smalltalk's excellent programming productivity.

RECAPPING THE SMALLTALK TERMINOLOGY

---

*The next best thing to knowing something
is knowing where to find it.*

SAMUEL JOHNSON

Before you go on to the next example, it might be useful to summarize all the operations you've done so far. Either skip ahead and refer to this section as you have specific questions, or read it now to brush up on the commands.

For each term listed below, the first line gives the name of the operation in Smalltalkese, the next line is the name of that operation in English, the third gives an example showing how to do it, the fourth indicates where examples are found in this book, and the last gives the appropriate sections of the User's Guide. The commands on the menu for text editing (middle-button menu in code windows), such as **cut** and **paste**, are defined in Appendix 1. The format here is:

Smalltalkese
  English (well, computerese)
    How to
      Examples in the text
        User's Guide Section

Accept a method
   Compile, link, and load a procedure
      Choose **accept** in the middle-button pop-up menu in
      area E of the browser
         Pages 24 and 31
            11.1 and 11.3

Add a category (also called **add protocol**)
   Create a place for a new bunch of procedures
      Choose **add protocol** in middle-button pop-menu in
      area C of the browser
         Pages 20 and 50.
            11.2

Add a class
   Add a new data type
      In area B of the browser, deselect any item that is selected
      by clicking it, then type and accept the new definition in
      area E
         Page 45
            12.1 to 12.3

Add a method
   Graft a procedure into the Smalltalk system
      Find the proper class and category in the browser, then type
      and accept the new method in area E
         Pages 19 to 25
            11.3

Browser
   The window used to find and modify Smalltalk methods
   (Not an action)
      Page 16
         5.4 and Chapter 9

Choose an item from a *fixed* menu
   Choose a command from a stationary list
      Move the cursor over the item in the list and click with the
      left button
         Pages 18, 19, and 25
            2.3 and 2.4

Choose an item from a *pop-up* menu
> Choose a command from a list that "pops up"
> > Hold down a button (middle or right), move cursor over item, and release the button
> > > Pages 17, 20, and 24
> > > > 1.3, 2.3, and 2.4

Class
> Like a data type, only better
> (Not an action)
> > Page 45
> > > 5.1 and Chapter 3 of the Blue Book*

Click
> Indicate an item or place
> > Press and release the left button
> > > Page 17
> > > > 1.1

Close a window
> Remove a window from the display
> > While in the window, choose **close** from the right-button pop-up menu
> > > Page 35
> > > > 2.5

Collection
> An object that holds a group of objects (**Strings** and **Arrays** are collections)
> > A specific class whose subclasses are the various kinds of collections
> > > Page 46
> > > > Chapter 9 of the Blue Book

---

* As mentioned in the preface, "Blue Book" refers to *Smalltalk-80: The Language and its Implementation* by Adele Goldberg and Dave Robson (Reading, MA: Addison-Wesley, 1983).

Deselect
>   In a fixed menu, make no item selected
>>   Click on the item that is currently selected
>>>   Page 31
>>>   2.3

do it
>   Run the piece of Smalltalk code that is selected, usually a call on a procedure with arguments
>>   Choose **do it** from the middle-button pop-up menu
>>>   Page 32
>>>   1.3 and 6.1

Editing
>   Editing (funny, that's the same in English)
>>   The editor is always available in any window you can type into
>>>   Pages 20 and 21
>>>   Appendix 1

Enter a window (also called "Select a view")
>   Make a window be the active window
>>   Move the cursor into the window and click with the left button
>>>   Pages 16 and 31
>>>   2.1 and 2.3

File in code
>   Bring Smalltalk class and method definitions into the system from a file
>>   In the System Workspace, modify a line in the Files section, select it, and choose **do it**
>>>   Page 42
>>>   22.3

File out code
>   Save Smalltalk code by writing it on a file in the file system
>>   In areas A, B, C, or D of the browser, choose **file out** from the middle-button menu
>>>   Page 41
>>>   22.1

Fixed menu
A list of choices that stays on the screen when no button is pressed
(See "Choose an item from a fixed menu")
Pages 18 and 24
2.3

Frame a window
Change the shape and/or location of a window
Choose **frame** from the right-button pop-up menu (see example in the text)
Page 51
1.3 and 2.2

Instance
One of the objects described by a class; it has memory and responds to messages
(Not an action)
Page 45
5.1 and Chapter 1 of the Blue Book

Message
A request for an object to carry out one of its procedures
(See "Send a message")
Page 12
5.1 and Chapter 1 of the Blue Book

Message selector
The name of a procedure (or of an operator)
(Not an action)
Page 11
Chapter 2 of the Blue Book

Method
A procedure—that is, the code that runs when a message is sent; it can also be thought of as a description of one of an object's operations
(Not an action)
Page 9
5.1 and Chapter 1 of the Blue Book

Object
>A package of data and procedures that belong together;
>the contents of any variable or constant is an object
>>(Not an action)
>>>Page 11
>>>>5.1 and Chapter 1 of the Blue Book

Pop-up menu
>A list of choices that appears when you press the middle or right
>button
>>(See "Choose an item from a pop-up menu")
>>>Pages 20 and 24
>>>>1.3 and 2.3

Receiver
>The object that was sent the current message
>>(See **self** below)
>>>Page 12
>>>>5.4 and Chapter 1 of the Blue Book

Scroll a window
>Move the contents of a window to see another part of it
>>(See example and pocket reference card)
>>>Page 17
>>>>2.3

Send a message
>Call a procedure—that is, ask an object (the receiver) to do an
>operation with some arguments and return a result
>>(Happens inside methods)
>>>Page 12
>>>>5.1 and Chapter 1 of the Blue Book

Select an item in a *fixed* menu
>(Means the same thing as "Choose an item from a fixed menu")
>>Move the cursor over the item in the list and click with the
>>left button
>>>Pages 18, 19, and 24
>>>>2.3 and 2.4

Select an item in a *pop-up* menu
> Move between the choices in a pop-up menu, but do not release the button
>> Hold down the middle or right mouse button and move around in the menu until the desired item shows in reverse video
>>> (Not mentioned in the text, but part of choosing an item from a pop-up menu)
>>> 2.3

Select text
> Indicate a piece of text upon which the next editing operation will act
>> Hold down the left mouse button, move until the text is reverse video, then release
>>> Page 23
>>> 3.1

self
> The local name for the object that received the message whose method we are in
>> Used to send another message to the same object that received this one
>>> Page 13
>>> 5.4 and Chapter 1 of the Blue Book

Spawn a new browser
> Ask for a specialized browser at another place on the screen
>> Choose **spawn** from a middle-button pop-up menu in any part of the browser (in License 1, choose **browse**)
>>> Page 51
>>> 9.4

5

ANIMATING THE PROGRAM

A SECOND CLASS

----

*For which of you, desiring to build a tower,
does not first sit down and count the cost,
whether he has enough to complete it?*
THE HOLY BIBLE, Revised Standard Version

If you have worked in the computing industry and have tried to convince management to follow your ideas, you know that while a written proposal is nice, a good demo really sells the project. One of the nice things about Smalltalk is that a good demo is easy to create. In this chapter we will improve our program by adding animation, which produces excellent demos. There are three kinds of animation commonly used in Smalltalk, and we will tackle the simplest kind first. Our program will use black rectangles to represent the disks, and they will travel in two dimensions on a white background (see Figure 5.1). In this first version, the movement of the disks will be jumpy, not smooth. In an exercise in Appendix 4, we will meet class OpaqueForm and use the follow:while: message to produce smooth movement. Dan Ingalls

Figure 5.1

wrote a more sophisticated animation package, but it is not uniformly available to Smalltalk users, so we will not cover this third kind of animation here.

In a conventional programming language, a single large program would manage the position on the screen of each of the disks. It would call a routine to display images of the disks. The Smalltalk style is to make each disk be an object, that is, a package of data and procedures that belong together. A disk object is responsible for keeping track of its position on the screen and for displaying itself. We want the object that represents the whole game—the single instance of **TowerOf-Hanoi**—to know almost nothing about animation. Thus we divided the Tower of Hanoi game into objects, and we are about to make an object-oriented version of the program. These objects are really rather familiar, and they are pictured in Figure 5.2.

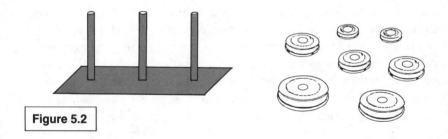

Figure 5.2

The definition for the class that represents the disks looks like this:

```
Object subclass: #HanoiDisk
    instanceVariableNames: 'name width pole rectangle '
    classVariableNames: 'TheTowers Thickness DiskGap '
    poolDictionaries: ''
    category: 'Kernel-Objects'
```

The definition of class **HanoiDisk** says that every disk owns four variables. Three additional variables are shared across the whole class. Their values can be read or written by any instance of the class. The comment in class **HanoiDisk** explains what the variables are for:

Each disk in the game is represented by an object of class HanoiDisk.
It has
   name--name of this disk (a Character)
   width--size of the disk (1 is the smallest disk width)
   pole--number telling which pole the disk is on
   rectangle--a rectangle on the screen that the disk occupies

There are three variables shared across the whole class
   TheTowers--the object that represents the whole game
      and holds the stacks of disks
   Thickness--the thickness of a disk in screen dots
   DiskGap--the number of screen dots between disks in a stack

We have just mentioned a distinction between two kinds of variables. An individual instance of class HanoiDisk represents one disk. It has its own distinct values for the "instance variables" called name, width, pole, and rectangle. For the entire class, there is just one value of each of the "class variables" called TheTowers, Thickness, and DiskGap. The single value of a class variable is shared by all instances of the class. Variables that are shared across the whole class are capitalized.

Local variables are another kind of variable we've discussed, and they are easy to understand. A local variable comes into being when a method begins execution, and goes away when the method terminates. Its name is meaningless outside of that individual method. The major difference between local and instance variables is that instance variables live as long as the objects of which they are a part, usually much longer than the execution of a single method. (Class variables live as long as the class is in existence, usually forever.)

As long as we are discussing variables, let's cover one last kind. A global variable is available anywhere in the system, and its name always begins with a capital letter. We have already seen many globals without knowing it. The way we access the object that represents a particular class, such as Array, is to use the global variable of the same name. In addition, there are a few globals whose values are not classes, such as Transcript.

Just to firm up the distinction between instance variables and class variables, let's look at the Pascal code that roughly corresponds to the definition of class HanoiDisk. (Keep in mind that we are really stretching things to make this analogy—don't get into any arguments with friends based on this.)

```
Program Hanoi
    Var TheTowers: TowerOfHanoi;
      Thickness:      Integer;
      DiskGap:        Integer;
    Record HanoiDisk =
      name:    Character;
      width:   Integer;
      pole:    Integer;
      rectangle:      Rectangle;
      end.
      . . .
```

Before we discuss the methods in class HanoiDisk, let's look at the changes to TowerOfHanoi. Although TowerOfHanoi knows nothing about the mechanics of the animation, it still needs a few changes. For example, it must create instances of HanoiDisk and push them onto the stacks instead of using characters. We could make changes directly to class TowerOfHanoi, but then we would not be able to run the old non-animated version of the game. Instead, let's define a new class that is a "subclass" of TowerOfHanoi. A subclass inherits all the definitions of variables and methods of the parent class. The subclass can add new variables, add new methods, and override old methods by redefining them. The class AnimatedTowerOfHanoi is declared as a subclass of TowerOfHanoi as follows:

```
TowerOfHanoi subclass: #AnimatedTowerOfHanoi
    instanceVariableNames: 'howMany  mockDisks '
    classVariableNames: ''
    poolDictionaries: ''
    category: 'Kernel-Objects'
```

The comment for this class is:

An object of this class represents the game. It inherits the variable stacks from class TowerOfHanoi. The new instance variables are:
   howMany--the number of disks
   mockDisks--an Array of fake disks (when a disk asks what disk
      it can move on top of, and the pole is empty, we return a mock disk;
      it has nearly infinite width)

The simplest way to explain the code in our two new classes is to consider first a move in the middle of the game. After we have looked at all the code in both classes for an average move, we will examine the initialization code. The actual moving of disks takes place during moveDisk:to:. Let's write a new version in class AnimatedTowerOfHanoi that overrides the one in TowerOfHanoi. Changes from the older version are underlined.

```
moveDisk: fromPin to: toPin
  | disk supportDisk |
  supportDisk ← (stacks at: toPin) isEmpty
    ifFalse: [(stacks at: toPin) first]
    ifTrue: [mockDisks at: toPin].
  disk ← (stacks at: fromPin) removeFirst.
  (stacks at: toPin) addFirst: disk.
  "inform the disk and show move"
  disk moveUpon: supportDisk.
"  Transcript cr.
  Transcript show: (fromPin printString, ' -> ', toPin printString, ' ').
  Transcript nextPut: disk name.
  Transcript endEntry. "
```

Starting in the middle of the method, the disk that is being moved (disk) is now an instance of HanoiDisk. When it is sent the message moveUpon:, it moves its image on the screen. The way it determines where to place itself is by looking at the disk it is moving on top of, supportDisk. When moved, a disk centers itself above a lower, supporting disk. What if the pole the disk is moving to is empty? The easiest way to handle this exceptional condition is to supply a fake disk as the supportDisk. The fake disk contains the pole number to move to and a position on the screen. The variable mockDisks is an array of three fake disks at the bases of the three poles. The new code at the beginning of the method

```
  supportDisk ← (stacks at: toPin) isEmpty
    ifFalse: [(stacks at: toPin) first]
    ifTrue: [mockDisks at: toPin].
```

assigns the proper mock disk to supportDisk if the stack is empty. If the stack has disks, the top disk is assigned to supportDisk.

We just used the message ifFalse:ifTrue:. The if-then-else control message comes in four flavors. The message ifTrue: executes the statements in the block if it was sent to the object true. If false was the receiver, control passes to the next statement in the program. Likewise, ifFalse: executes the block when sent to false. The message ifTrue:ifFalse: executes just one of its two blocks, depending on the conditional expression it was sent to. Finally, ifFalse:ifTrue: does exactly the same thing, but is simply written with the other block first. (Both forms are provided so that you can write whichever half you think of first.)

At the bottom of the method moveDisk:to: we modified the printing code to show the name of the disk (disk used to be just a character).

We will define the method name in HanoiDisk to allow each disk to return the character that is its name. We enclosed the entire printing code in comment quotes so that printing in the transcript window will not interrupt the animation. (For debugging, the comment quotes can be removed.)

The method moveUpon: is defined in class HanoiDisk and looks like this:

```
moveUpon: destination
  "This disk just moved. Record the new pole and tell the user."
  pole ← destination pole.
  "remove the old image"
  self invert.
  "reposition"
  rectangle center: destination center − (0 @ (Thickness + DiskGap)).
  "display the new one"
  self invert.
  (Delay forMilliseconds: 300) wait
```

In the assignment statement, we set this disk's new pole to be the destination disk's pole. The message pole, sent to the destination disk, asks what pole it is on. Next, we send ourselves the message invert to "exclusive or" our rectangle onto the screen.* This removes our image at the disk's old location. In the next line, we assign our rectangle a new center point. Then we invert again to place an image on the screen at the new location, and then pause for 300 milliseconds. Since pole and rectangle are instance variables, they retain their new values until we decide to move this disk again.

Before we plunge into the code for positioning disks, we need to discuss the coordinate system and the objects that stand for points and rectangles. The point (0,0) is at the upper left corner of the screen. The X axis goes across and the *positive* Y coordinates go down the screen, implying an upside-down coordinate system. The arithmetic operator @ makes a point out of two integers. Thus the expression 100@300 returns a point (an instance of class Point) whose X value is 100 and whose Y value is 300. This point is 100 screen dots out from the left edge and 300 dots down. Strictly speaking, in the expression 100@300, object 100 is an instance of SmallInteger (an integer) and it understands the message @, which has one argument. The @ method creates a new Point, and assigns it X and Y values. Points understand most arithmetic operations, such as +, −, *, //, =, and abs. (// means divide and truncate to an integer. abs means take the absolute value.)

---

* The operation "exclusive or" on two rectangles combines their contents to produce a third. It puts black where the bits in the two rectangles are different, and white where they are the same. 1 bits represent black and 0 bits are white, so the bitwise operation is exclusive or.

Let's examine the code for repositioning the rectangle.

rectangle center: destination center − (0 @ (Thickness + DiskGap)).

A Rectangle is a bundle of four points that are the corners of a rectangle. We will compute our rectangle's new center by subtracting a quantity from the destination disk's center. (Subtracting a positive quantity means moving up on the screen.) Thickness + DiskGap is the spacing between disk centers. 0 @ (Thickness + DiskGap) creates a point whose X is 0 and whose Y value is the height of a disk. Subtraction between points is "vector subtraction," and yields a new point whose Y is the difference between the two points' Y values. The message center: moves our disk's rectangle to a new location without changing its size. Note that there are two very similar message names, center and center:. They have the same name except for the colon. There is an informal convention among Smalltalk programmers that pairs of messages like center and center: are related. The one without the colon asks for a value and the one with the colon sets the value.

Definitions of the classes Point and Rectangle are found in the System Browser in the category **Graphics-Primitives**, which is the first **Graphics-** category. The blue Smalltalk book explains the full story of Points and Rectangles in Chapter 18.

We still have some messages for class HanoiDisk that have not been defined. These are used in moveUpon:.

pole
    "return which pole this disk is on"
    ↑ pole

Every Smalltalk method that runs returns a single object as its result. If you don't specify anything to be returned, the object that received the message (self) is returned. To return some other object, put an up-arrow, ↑ , in front of the expression for the object you want to return. In this case, the whole purpose of the method is to return this disk's pole number, so that another disk can compare its pole number with it.

center
    "return a Point that is the current center of this disk"
    ↑ rectangle center

Note that center (without the colon) is already a message in class Rectangle. Any rectangle that receives it computes and returns its center point.

Alas, the message center: (with the colon) is not defined as "standard equipment" in class **Rectangle**. One virtue of Smalltalk is that the user can correct oversights in the basic system. When we type in the methods for class **HanoiDisk** into the system, we will have to correct this oversight. We will make an excursion up to class **Rectangle** and define the message **center:** as

```
center: thePoint      | extent |
    "move the rectangle so it is centered on the point,
        but keep the width and height unchanged"
    extent ← corner − origin.
    origin ← thePoint − (extent // 2).
    corner ← origin + extent
```

An instance of class **Rectangle** only stores two points internally: the upper left and the lower right point. It computes the remaining points if they are needed. The message **center:** takes a single argument and stores it in **thePoint**. The goal is to move the rectangle so that its new center point is **thePoint**. We save the size of the rectangle in the local variable **extent**. The new upper left-hand corner (**origin**) is the center minus one-half the extent. The new lower right-hand corner (**corner**) is the origin plus the extent. (Systems programming was never so easy.)

The code for **moveUpon:** sends another message that we have not defined. Here is the code to "exclusive or" the image of a disk onto the screen:

```
invert
    "show a disk on the screen by turning white to black in a
        rectangular region "
    Display reverse: rectangle
```

Now let's look at the initialization code for the animated version of our game. A new version of **hanoi** in class **AnimatedTowerOfHanoi** will override the one in **TowerOfHanoi**.

```
hanoi      | aString |
    "Ask the user how many disks, set up the game, and move disks until
        we are done."
    aString ← FillInTheBlank request: 'Please type the number of
disks in the tower, and <cr>'.
    howMany ← aString asNumber.
    self setUpDisks.      "create the disks and stacks"

    self moveTower: howMany from: 1 to: 3 using: 2.

    " (AnimatedTowerOfHanoi new) hanoi "
```

The first difference is that the number of disks in the game is now stored in howMany instead of height. height was a temporary variable (indicated by its appearing between vertical bars at the beginning of the method). Its value was not accessible to methods that were called several levels below hanoi. We have made howMany an instance variable so that any disk can ask for it later (see below). Second, we have moved all of the initialization of the stacks of disks into a new subroutine called setUpDisks.

```
setUpDisks      | disk displayBox |
    "Create the disks and set up the poles."
    "Tell all disks what game they are in and set disk thickness and gap"
    HanoiDisk new whichTowers: self.
    displayBox ← 20@100 corner: 380@320.
    Display white: displayBox.
    Display border: displayBox width: 2.
    "The poles are an array of three stacks. Each stack is an
        OrderedCollection."
    stacks ← (Array new: 3) collect: [:each | OrderedCollection new].
    howMany to: 1 by: −1 do: [:size |
        disk ← HanoiDisk new width: size pole: 1. "Create a disk"
        (stacks at: 1) addFirst: disk.      "Push it onto a stack"
        disk invert "show on the screen"].

    "When a pole has no disk on it, one of these mock disks acts as a bottom
        disk. A moving disk will ask a mock disk its width and pole number"
    mockDisks ← Array new: 3.
    1 to: 3 do: [:index |
        mockDisks at: index put: (HanoiDisk new width: 1000 pole: index)].
```

Undaunted by the size of this method, let's examine its parts.

```
    HanoiDisk new whichTowers: self.
```

Class HanoiDisk has three variables that are shared class-wide: TheTowers, Thickness, and DiskGap. Later, we will define the message whichTowers: to initialize them. It only has to be sent once, and this seems like a good place to do it.

The next statement creates a white area with a black border on the screen in which we will put the images of our disks.

```
    displayBox ← 20@100 corner: 380@320.
    Display white: displayBox.
    Display border: displayBox width: 2.
```

We specify the area to make white by creating a rectangle. The message corner: sent to a Point causes it to create a new instance of class Rectangle. In this case, its upper left point (20,100) receives the message and takes the lower right point (380,320) as an argument.

Display is a global variable that holds the object that represents the screen. It is an instance of DisplayScreen and inherits much of its behavior from the basic classes that represent bit images: Form, DisplayMedium, and DisplayObject. The BitBlt operation actually moves images around. Chapters 18, 19, and 20 of the Blue Book explain these classes, BitBlt, and displaying in general.

The message white: is one member of a family of rectangle-filling methods. The others are black:, gray:, lightGray:, darkGray:, and very-LightGray:. We place a black border two dots wide inside the white rectangle by sending the message border:width: to Display. To display more complicated images, one generally creates an instance of class Form, makes an image inside of it, and transfers the image in the Form to the display. A Form can be treated like a brush, and moved along a path, such as a line or a curve.

The next section of code hasn't changed much:

```
stacks ← (Array new: 3) collect: [:each | OrderedCollection new].
howMany to: 1 by: − 1 do: [:size |
    disk ← HanoiDisk new width: size pole: 1. "Create a disk"
    (stacks at: 1) addFirst: disk.        "Push it onto a stack"
    disk invert "show on the screen"].
```

stacks is an array of three stacks. We fill the first stack in reverse order with instances of HanoiDisk. Each new instance of HanoiDisk is immediately sent the message width:pole: to set its width and which pole it is on. Inside width:pole: the disk's name and rectangle are set. In the last line we tell the disk to display itself.

We are ready for the final part of setUpDisks.

```
mockDisks ← Array new: 3.
1 to: 3 do: [:index |
    mockDisks at: index put: (HanoiDisk new width: 1000 pole: index)].
```

The mock disks are the fake disks used by moveDisk:to: to represent poles that do not have any disks on them. There is one for each pole and it is located just below where the first disk would go. We give the mock disks a width of 1000 to make them so wide that any disk can move on top of them, using the normal rules of the game. The message at:put: stores a value in a particular place in an Array. The first argument is the index within the Array and the second argument is the value to be stored. The message at: retrieves the value from the location in the Array specified by the argument.

At the beginning of setUpDisks, the statement HanoiDisk new whichTowers: self initialized the class variables in HanoiDisk. Here is the code:

```
whichTowers: aTowerOfHanoi
   "Install the object representing the towers"
   TheTowers ← aTowerOfHanoi.
   Thickness ← 14.      "thickness of a disk in screen dots"
   DiskGap ← 2.      "distance between disks"
```

It is clear why all disks need to know a thickness and a distance from other disks on a stack, but the purpose of TheTowers is less clear. Communication is crucial between AnimatedTowerOfHanoi and the disks. They communicate by sending messages to each other. If the main program wants to ask a disk something like, "How wide are you?", it asks the appropriate disk object on one of the stacks. If, on the other hand, a disk trying to position itself on the screen needs to ask the object that represents the whole game a question, what does it call that object? The variable TheTowers holds the instance of TowerOfHanoi. A disk can say TheTowers howMany to ask the instance of Animated-TowerOfHanoi how many disks there are total. At the beginning of setUpDisks in the statement (HanoiDisk new whichTowers: self), self is the object representing the whole game. That object is stored into aTowerOfHanoi and then into TheTowers.

Now let's examine the initialization code for a HanoiDisk.

```
width: size pole: whichPole      | where y |
   "set the values for this disk"
   width ← size.
   pole ← whichPole.
   "compute the center of the disk on the screen"
   size >= 1000 ifFalse: ["a normal disk"
         name ← Character value: ($A asciiValue) + size − 1.
         y ← 300 − ((TheTowers howMany − size)*(Thickness + DiskGap)).
         where ← 100@y]
      ifTrue: ["a mock disk"
         name ← $m.
         where ← (100*whichPole) @ (300 + Thickness + DiskGap)].
   "create the rectangle, specify its size, and locate its center"
   rectangle ← 0@0 extent: (size*14)@Thickness.
   rectangle center: where.
```

First we set the disk's own **width** and **pole**. We are actually creating two different kinds of disks. Mock disks will not show on the screen, but real disks will use the locations of the centers of mock disks to stack themselves in the right places. Regular disks have both a width and a position on the first pole that depend on their size. The message "greater than or equal to" is written as >=. A normal disk gets a computed value for its **name**, and a mock disk gets the character m.

Next we compute the local variable **where** to hold the position of the disk. We'll put the three stacks at X positions of 100, 200, and 300. The bottoms of all stacks will be at 300 in Y. N*(Thickness + DiskGap) is the height of N disks. Inside class HanoiDisk, we don't know the total number of disks. To find that out, we must ask TheTower, because it holds all of the game-wide information. (TheTowers howMany − size)*(Thickness + DiskGap) is the distance above the base of the stack of a disk with width size. The bottom disk is the widest and the top disk is the narrowest (with size = 1). Given the size, these two statements create a point, **where**, for the center of a normal disk.

```
y ← 300 − ((TheTowers howMany − size)*(Thickness + DiskGap)).
where ← 100@y.
```

If a disk's **size** >= 1000, then the disk is a mock disk. Its position is below the start of a stack, and the stack for each pole is in a different place. Here is a mock disk's location:

```
where ← (100*whichPole) @ (300 + Thickness + DiskGap).
```

The statement

```
rectangle ← 0@0 extent: (size*14)@Thickness.
```

creates a Rectangle at (0,0) with the proper width and height. The final statement

```
rectangle center: where.
```

moves the Rectangle so that its center is at the point we computed.

We have called the method howMany in AnimatedTowerOfHanoi, but we have neglected to define it. The code simply returns the value we saved in an instance variable.

```
howMany
"return the number of disks"
↑ howMany
```

We've seen a lot of new things in this chapter: class variables, objects of two different classes interacting, and a class that is a subclass of another one. All the code we looked at may seem a bit confusing now, but it will become more coherent after you get it into the browser.

INSTALLING THE CLASSES HanoiDisk AND AnimatedTowerOfHanoi

Your screen probably has two browsers on it, a Class Browser for TowerOfHanoi and the original System Browser. Let's create class HanoiDisk first and do it in the System Browser. Enter the System Browser and deselect anything that is selected in area B (see Figure 5.3).

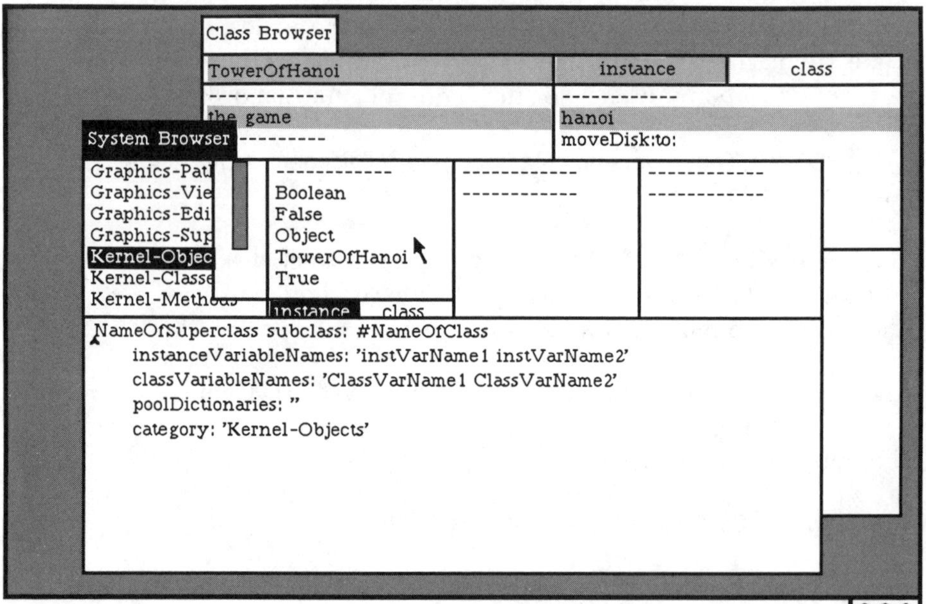

Figure 5.3

Modify the template in area E to be:

```
Object subclass: #HanoiDisk
    instanceVariableNames: 'name width pole rectangle '
    classVariableNames: 'TheTowers Thickness DiskGap '
    poolDictionaries: ''
    category: 'Kernel-Objects'
```

accept and move to area B. Choose **comment** from the middle-button menu and install this class comment. (Once again, if your system is a License 1 system, be sure to put the comment inside the single quotes in area E.)

Each disk in the game is represented by an object of class HanoiDisk. It has
    name--name of this disk (a Character)
    width--size of the disk (1 is the smallest disk width)
    pole--number telling which pole the disk is on
    rectangle--a rectangle on the screen that the disk occupies

There are three variables shared across the whole class
    TheTowers--the object that represents the whole game
        and holds the stacks of disks
    Thickness--the thickness of a disk in screen dots
    DiskGap--the number of screen dots between disks in a stack

    accept, then choose **protocols** from the middle-button menu in area B. We will divide the messages in class HanoiDisk into two groups called **access** and **moving**. Type this in area E and **accept**.

('access')
('moving')

    Let's enter the methods in the **access** category. In area C, select **access** and type and **accept** each of these methods individually in area E.

pole
    "return which pole this disk is on"
    ↑ pole

The character ↑ is usually on the ∧ key (shift 6).

name
    "return the name of this disk"
    ↑ name

---

whichTowers: aTowerOfHanoi
    "Install the object representing the towers"
    TheTowers ← aTowerOfHanoi.
    Thickness ← 14.   "thickness of a disk in screen dots"
    DiskGap ← 2.   "distance between disks"

    Anytime that you want to see the class definition again (to remind yourself what the instance variables are named), you can choose **defi-**

nition from the middle-button menu in area B. Back in the **access** category, define the method for width:pole: as follows:

```
width: size pole: whichPole    | where y |
    "set the values for this disk"
    width ← size.
    pole ← whichPole.
    "compute the center of the disk on the screen"
    size >= 1000 ifFalse: ["a normal disk"
        name ← Character value: ($A asciiValue) + size − 1.
        y ← 300 − ((TheTowers howMany − size)*(Thickness + DiskGap)).
        where ← 100@y]
      ifTrue: ["a mock disk"
        name ← $m.
        where ← (100*whichPole) @ (300 + Thickness + DiskGap)].
    "create the rectangle, specify its size, and locate its center"
    rectangle ← 0@0 extent: (size*14)@Thickness.
    rectangle center: where.
```

When you **accept**, the compiler may put up a menu to ask you if howMany is a new method name. If so, click on **proceed as is** (or on the item **howMany**, if it appears)*. Now let's continue by replacing the contents of area E with the following method:

```
center
    "return a Point that is the current center of this disk"
    ↑ rectangle center
```

Now we need to go to class Rectangle and add the message **center:**. After accepting the message you just typed in area E, go up to area A. Scroll up the list of categories in area A until you see **Graphics-Primi-tives**. It is the uppermost category of the **Graphics-** type. Select it, then select Rectangle in area B and **accessing** in area C. In area E replace the template with:

```
center: thePoint   | extent |
    "move the rectangle so it is centered on the point,
      but keep the width and height unchanged"
    extent ← corner − origin.
    origin ← thePoint − (extent // 2).
    corner ← origin + extent
```

---

* In some systems, the compiler will also ask you to confirm center: as a new message.

accept it and then scroll back in area A to Kernel-Objects. Select it, then select HanoiDisk, then select moving. Now we'll fill in the methods that have to do with moving disks.

```
moveUpon: destination
    "This disk just moved. Record the new pole and tell the user."
    pole ← destination pole.
    "remove the old image"
    self invert.
    "reposition"
    rectangle center: destination center − (0 @ (Thickness + DiskGap)).
    "display the new one"
    self invert.
    (Delay forMilliseconds: 300) wait
```

The compiler will fret because invert is an unfamiliar message name. Gently reassure it by clicking on **proceed as is** (choose the name of the method if you are using a License 1 system from Apple).

```
invert
    "show a disk on the screen by turning white to black in a
        rectangular region "
    Display reverse: rectangle
```

Let's create class AnimatedTowerOfHanoi in the System Browser and copy methods from the Class Browser for TowerOfHanoi. Enter the System Browser and deselect anything that is selected in area B.

Edit the template in area E until it looks like this:

```
TowerOfHanoi subclass: #AnimatedTowerOfHanoi
    instanceVariableNames: 'howMany mockDisks '
    classVariableNames: ' '
    poolDictionaries: "
    category: 'Kernel-Objects'
```

After you've accepted that, set the comment to be:

```
An object of this class represents the game. It inherits the variable stacks
from class TowerOfHanoi. The new instance variables are
    howMany--the number of disks
    mockDisks--an Array of fake disks (when a disk asks what disk
        it can move on top of, and the pole is empty, we return a mock disk;
        it has nearly infinite width)
```

accept and move up to area B. Choose **protocols** from the middle-button menu and replace the contents of area E with

----

('the game')

and **accept**. In area C, be sure that **the game** is selected. Then type
and **accept** each of these methods individually in area E. (If you wish,
go to the other browser and copy the hanoi method and then modify
it.)

```
hanoi      | aString |
   "Ask the user how many disks, set up the game, and move disks until
      we are done."
   aString ← FillInTheBlank request: 'Please type the number of
disks in the tower, and <cr>'.
   howMany ← aString asNumber.
   self setUpDisks.      "create the disks and stacks"

   self moveTower: howMany from: 1 to: 3 using: 2.

   " (AnimatedTowerOfHanoi new) hanoi "
```

The compiler will become suspicious of the message setUpDisks.
Tell it to stop being so stuffy by choosing **proceed as is** (choose the
name of the method if you are using a License 1 system from Apple).
Now type and **accept** the method:

```
setUpDisks      | disk displayBox |
   "Create the disks and set up the poles."
   "Tell all disks what game they are in and set disk thickness and gap"
   HanoiDisk new whichTowers: self.
   displayBox ← 20@100 corner: 380@320.
   Display white: displayBox.
   Display border: displayBox width: 2.
   "The poles are an array of three stacks. Each stack is an
      OrderedCollection."
   stacks ← (Array new: 3) collect: [:each | OrderedCollection new].
   howMany to: 1 by: −1 do: [:size |
      disk ← HanoiDisk new width: size pole: 1.      "Create a disk"
      (stacks at: 1) addFirst: disk.      "Push it onto a stack"
      disk invert "show on the screen"].

   "When a pole has no disk on it, one of these mock disks acts as a bottom
      disk. A moving disk will ask a mock disk its width and pole number"
   mockDisks ← Array new: 3.
   1 to: 3 do: [:index |
      mockDisks at: index put: (HanoiDisk new width: 1000 pole: index)].
```

Go to the **Class Browser** and copy the moveDisk:to: method, bring it into this category, and then modify it as shown by the underlining below:

```
moveDisk: fromPin to: toPin
    | disk supportDisk |
    supportDisk ← (stacks at: toPin) isEmpty
        ifFalse: [(stacks at: toPin) first]
        ifTrue: [mockDisks at: toPin].
    disk ← (stacks at: fromPin) removeFirst.
    (stacks at: toPin) addFirst: disk.
    "inform the disk and show move"
    disk moveUpon: supportDisk.
"   Transcript cr.
    Transcript show: (fromPin printString, ' − > ', toPin printString, ' ').
    Transcript nextPut: disk name.
    Transcript endEntry. "
```

```
howMany
    "return the number of disks"
    ↑ howMany
```

We are finished entering AnimatedTowerOfHanoi. Let's replace the Class Browser for TowerOfHanoi with one for AnimatedTowerOfHanoi. Enter the Class Browser, and choose **close** from the right-button menu. Back in the System Browser, go to area B and choose **spawn** (**browse** in License 1 systems) from the middle-button menu. Position the corner cursors to frame your new browser.

Now let's see some moving disks! Remember to accept the method you just typed. Enter the Class Browser for AnimatedTowerOfHanoi, go to the hanoi method, and scroll to the comment at the bottom of the code. Select (AnimatedTowerOfHanoi new) hanoi, and choose **do it**. See the section "Troubleshooting Runtime Errors" in Chapter 3 if the program has bugs (see Figure 5.4).

Notice that the white area in which the animation is running is not really a window. Our program wrote on the screen directly, without enclosing the drawing in a window that can become active after it has been covered up. In order to keep this example simple, we will not discuss how to create a new kind of window. (Later, when you have finished this book, you can examine the classes in the category **Interface-File Model** and use them as an example.)

You now have some experience with graphics in Smalltalk. One of

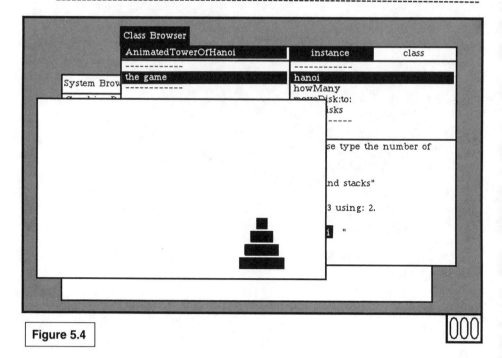

Figure 5.4

the exercises in Appendix 4 explores a smoother and fancier kind of animation.

The class AnimatedTowerOfHanoi is a subclass of TowerOfHanoi, from which it inherits instance variables and methods. In this chapter, we have used inheritance (also called subclassing) in all three of the ways it is used in Smalltalk. First, we used it to add to the behavior of a class, TowerOfHanoi, by adding instance variables, overriding existing methods, and adding new methods. Second, we used subclassing as a protection mechanism. While the animation code was "in pieces on the floor" being written and debugged, our previous example in TowerOfHanoi still worked. All of the changes and new code were isolated in the subclass, leaving the original class untouched. The third use of inheritance was illustrated when we created class TowerOfHanoi in the previous chapter. Making a subclass is the only way to make a new class in Smalltalk. The greatest independence a new class can have is to be a subclass of class Object. In that case, all it inherits is "object-ness," that is, the property of being an object in the Smalltalk system.

6

AN ALGORITHM FOR
THE REST OF US

MOVE A DISK BY MOVING AN OBJECT

---

*What is one and one and one and one
and one and one and one and one and one
and one?*

        THE WHITE QUEEN TO ALICE in *Through the
Looking Glass*, Chapter 9

Lewis Carroll's joke would not be funny to a computer. A computer would simply add up the "ones" and get the right answer, while a person loses track after the fourth or fifth one. The recursive solution to the Tower of Hanoi is just as bad as the White Queen's math problem. Our programs in the previous chapters have determined what move to make by permuting pole numbers that were stored "on the stack." Each recursive call on **moveTower:from:to:using:** uses the values of the input parameters from the previous call to choose a move. This is fine for computers, but you have probably noticed that we humans have a "stack" that forgets when too many things are pushed onto it. No human would ever solve the tower puzzle the same way the recursive algorithm does. Let's switch the program over to an algorithm that any person could use to solve the Tower of Hanoi. Besides using a more intuitive algorithm, we hope in this section to demonstrate what objects are really for, and to show you a program that is simpler in Smalltalk than in Pascal, C, or LISP.

Here are some simple rules that any person can use to solve the Tower of Hanoi:

(1) Don't make illegal moves (always put a small disk on top of a bigger disk).
(2) Don't move the disk you just moved (the last move should not be undone).
(3) If there are two legal moves, choose the one that does not put a disk back on the pole it came from the last time it moved (make forward progress).

This is much more like it! We won't offer a proof that these rules represent a mathematically airtight solution, but they do work. The three rules are heuristics based on practical experience. We are going to write a program that implements these three rules. Please don't confuse this with "rule-based programming." Smalltalk is not a system that takes rules as source code, as a "production system language" does.

The first two rules are easy. The third rule requires you to remember which pole each disk came from the last time it moved. That's a little bit of a strain, but we do have a computer here to help us. Clearly, each disk should have a variable to store the pole it last moved from. In addition, the new algorithm needs to remember what disk moved last, what disk we are considering moving next, and what disk we are thinking of as a possible destination.

In spite of the fact that we are completely changing the algorithm, the data structures stay almost exactly the same as before. We will divide the problem up into objects exactly as before, but we will use two new classes. Class TowerByRules represents the whole game and holds all the game-wide information. Each disk is an instance of class HanoiDiskRules. We would like our new program to be animated, and since the knowledge of animation in class HanoiDisk has nothing to do with the algorithm for deciding what disk to move, we will use most of HanoiDisk unchanged. In the last chapter we made class Animated-TowerOfHanoi be a subclass of TowerOfHanoi. It inherited instance variables and messages. In the same way, TowerByRules will be a subclass of AnimatedTowerOfHanoi and HanoiDiskRules will be a subclass of HanoiDisk.

We are building up quite a large inheritance chain, so let's look at it explicitly.

```
Object ()
  TowerOfHanoi ('stacks' )
    AnimatedTowerOfHanoi ('howMany' 'mockDisks' )
      TowerByRules ('oldDisk' 'currentDisk' 'destinationDisk' )
```

Here we see TowerByRules with its newly added instance variables. It inherits behavior and instance variables from Animated-TowerOfHanoi, which in turn inherits from TowerOfHanoi, which inherits from Object.

```
Object ()
  HanoiDisk ('width' 'pole' 'rectangle' 'name' )
    HanoiDiskRules ('previousPole' )
```

HanoiDiskRules is a subclass of HanoiDisk and adds a single new instance variable. These two subclass tables can be seen in the browser. After we enter the two new classes in the next section, you can select a class in area B, and then choose **heirarchy** from the middle-button menu. Here is the definition of class TowerByRules:

```
AnimatedTowerOfHanoi subclass: #TowerByRules
  instanceVariableNames: 'oldDisk currentDisk destinationDisk'
  classVariableNames: ''
  poolDictionaries: ''
  category: 'Kernel-Objects'
```

Here is the comment for TowerByRules:

An object of this class represents the game. It holds an array of stacks that hold disks. It also keeps track of which disk just moved and which disk should move next. The new instance variables are
    oldDisk--the disk that was moved last time
    currentDisk--we are considering moving this disk
    destinationDisk--and putting it on top of this disk

The instance variables stacks, howMany, and mockDisks are the same as before. At the beginning of a move, we know oldDisk, the disk that moved last time. If we can pick a currentDisk and destinationDisk that satisfy the three rules, the rest is easy. This suggests a "main loop" to find the next move, and we will put it in the hanoi method.

```
hanoi
    "Ask the user how many disks, set up the game, and move disks until
        we are done."
    howMany ← (FillInTheBlank request: 'Please type the number of
disks in the tower, and <cr>') asNumber.
    self setUpDisks.      "create the disks and stacks"


    "Iterate until all disks are on one tower again."
    ["decide which to move and also set destinationDisk"
    currentDisk ← self decide.
    "remove the disk and put it on the new pole"
    (stacks at: currentDisk pole) removeFirst.
    (stacks at: destinationDisk pole) addFirst: currentDisk.
    "tell the disk where it is now"
    currentDisk moveUpon: destinationDisk.
    oldDisk ← currentDisk.      "get ready for the next move"
    self allOnOneTower] whileFalse.      "test if done"

    "(TowerByRules new) hanoi "
```

The entire second half of the method is a "while loop." The statement

[*statements. a boolean expression*] whileFalse.

executes the statements repeatedly until the boolean expression is true.
(In Smalltalk's terminology, the code inside the square brackets is a
block of unevaluated code. The block is an object and it is sent the
message whileFalse. It executes itself repeatedly until the last expression in the block has a value of true.)

Let's consider what needs to be done to make a move in the middle of the game. Starting with the disk that just finished moving, decide
which other disk to move next and where to put it. Move the disk by
transferring it from one stack to another and altering the disk's internal
state (its location). When all disks are on one pole, we are done; otherwise start again on a new move.

Now let's look at the code in more detail. Inside the whileFalse
loop in hanoi, the first statement

currentDisk ← self decide.

does all the work of determining which disk to move, and, as a side
effect, sets destinationDisk to be the disk onto which currentDisk will
move. The method decide uses the three rules to choose the next disk
to move. To do this, decide ignores the disk that just finished moving
and considers the disks on top of the other two poles. It tests to see if

they have any legal moves. If one does, decide chooses its best move (in case it can move to two places) by invoking Rule 3. It sets destinationDisk to be the disk that the moving disk will land on top of, and returns the object that represents the moving disk.

```
decide
    "use the last disk moved (oldDisk) to find a new disk to move
        (currentDisk) and a disk to put it on top of (destinationDisk)"
    self topsOtherThan: oldDisk do: [:movingDisk |
        movingDisk hasLegalMove ifTrue:
        ["remember the disk upon which to move"
        destinationDisk ← movingDisk bestMove.
        ↑ movingDisk      "return the disk that moves"]].
```

The entire method is one long statement: a rather odd control structure named topsOtherThan:do:. Most computer languages give you a few standard control structures such as if-then-else, for-loops, and repeat-until; and that's all you get. In Smalltalk, you can write your own control methods and use them to direct the flow of control in programs. The method topsOtherThan:do: accepts two arguments. The first is oldDisk, the disk that will not be moving. The second is a block of code enclosed in square brackets. The block is of the form

   [:movingDisk | *statements*].

The block of code is not evaluated when the message topsOtherThan:do: is sent, but is an object which contains unevaluated code and is handed as an argument to the method topsOtherThan:do:. The block contains a local variable, movingDisk. The colon before movingDisk means that movingDisk's value will be assigned at the time the block runs. As you might expect, the block is run once for each of the disks that is a candidate to move, and the object that represents that disk is assigned to movingDisk.* The message topsOtherThan:do: is sent to self, so when we write the code for topsOtherThan:do:, we will put it in class TowerByRules, where the decide method is located. The statement inside the block is

```
    movingDisk hasLegalMove ifTrue:
    ["remember the disk upon which to move"
    destinationDisk ← movingDisk bestMove.
    ↑ movingDisk   "return the disk that moves"]
```

---

* *LISP* programmers note that a block is like *(LAMBDA(movingDisk) statements)*. Pascal programmers note that it is like a local procedure of one argument.

The method hasLegalMove returns true if movingDisk fits on top of any other pole. If so, destinationDisk is assigned the result sending the message bestMove to movingDisk. It answers with one of the two disks it could move upon. destinationDisk is an instance variable of Tower-ByRules, so it is available inside the hanoi method when this method returns (we'd like to return multiple values here, both destinationDisk and movingDisk, but Smalltalk does not provide for easy returning of multiple values). The expression ↑ movingDisk forces control to leave the loop, terminates this message, and returns the value that worked for movingDisk.

The messages decide and hanoi were both in class TowerByRules. Since hasLegalMove is a message that is sent to an individual disk, the method is in class HanoiDiskRules. Lets look at class HanoiDiskRules. It is a subclass of HanoiDisk.

```
HanoiDisk subclass: #HanoiDiskRules
  instanceVariableNames: ' previousPole '
  classVariableNames: ''
  poolDictionaries: ''
  category: 'Kernel-Objects'
```

Only the new instance variable, previousPole, is mentioned. Each instance of HanoiDiskRules also has the variables name, width, pole, and rectangle that it inherits from HanoiDisk. Here is the comment:

```
previousPole--number of the pole this disk was on previously
```

And the code for hasLegalMove is

```
hasLegalMove
  "Do either of the other two poles have a top disk large enough for
    this disk to rest on?"
  TheTowers polesOtherThan: self do: [:targetDisk |
    "when a pole has no disk, targetDisk is a mock disk with infinite width"
    width < targetDisk width ifTrue: [ ↑ true]].
  ↑ false
```

Once again TheTowers is the object that represents the whole game, in this case an instance of TowerByRules. It is being sent the message polesOtherThan:do:, which looks suspiciously like the message tops-OtherThan:do: in decide. (Notice that topsOtherThan:do: was sent to self. Inside decide, self was a TowerByRules, but here self is a disk, so we must send it to TheTowers.)

Looking again at the code for hasLegalMove, we see a new control structure. polesOtherThan:do: is just like topsOtherThan:do: except for the way it treats poles that have no disks on them. In decide we looked for disks that would move, so an empty pole was of no interest. The local variable targetDisk can be either a real disk or something that stands for an empty pole. As before we'll use a mock disk to stand for the top disk on an empty pole. The message polesOtherThan:do: executes the block that it gets as its second argument once for each of the other two poles. If the pole has a stack of disks, the top disk is assigned to the block's local variable. If the pole is empty, the mock disk for that pole is assigned to targetDisk.

```
width < targetDisk width ifTrue: [ ↑ true]
```

Inside the loop, targetDisk is the top disk on a pole other than self's (movingDisk's) pole, and we test to see if self can legally move there. The variable width is self's own width. The second mention of width is a message to targetDisk, asking it to return its width. If self's width is less, then return true. If both other poles have been tested by poles-OtherThan:do: and no move was legal, the next statement, ↑ false, informs the caller that self cannot make a legal move.

Since we mentioned the message width, let's define it.

```
width
    "Return the size of this disk"
    ↑ width
```

Each instance of HanoiDiskRules responds to the message width by returning the value of its variable called width. It is common practice to define a message with a name that is the same as an instance variable name. By informal convention, the message width returns the value of the variable width.

Now we come to the question of computing the best move if a disk has two possible moves. Rule 3 says that a disk should not move back to the pole from which it last moved. Each disk has a variable, previousPole, that holds the number of its previous pole. In the method decide, we wrote

```
destinationDisk ← movingDisk bestMove.
```

Like hasLegalMove, bestMove is a message sent to movingDisk, and like hasLegalMove it must look at each of the possible places that moving-Disk can go.

```
bestMove      | secondBest |
   "If self can move two places, which is best? Return the top disk of
      the pole that this disk has not been on recently."
   TheTowers polesOtherThan: self do: [:targetDisk |
      width < targetDisk width ifTrue:
      [secondBest ← targetDisk.
      targetDisk pole = previousPole ifFalse: [ ↑ targetDisk]]].
   ↑ secondBest "as a last resort, return a pole it was on recently"
```

For each other pole, see if self will fit on the top disk. If so, remember this disk in the local variable secondBest (we may need it). If the new pole is not this disk's previous pole, then return targetDisk. If, instead, the only legal move puts the disk back to its previous pole, return that move (the value of secondBest). The code for the message pole is inherited from HanoiDisk.

Now that we've covered everything in the decide method, let's see how the two custom control structures are defined in TowerBy-Rules.

```
topsOtherThan: thisDisk do: aBlock
   "Evaluate the block of code using the top disk on each of the other
      two poles. If a pole is empty, ignore it. This is for actual disks."
   1 to: 3 do: [:aPole |
      "If the pole does not have thisDisk and is not empty, then
         execute aBlock"
      (aPole ~= thisDisk pole) & ((stacks at: aPole) isEmpty not) ifTrue:
         [aBlock value: (stacks at: aPole) first "execute the block"]]
```

For each of the three poles, if it is not thisDisk's pole and if the stack on the pole is not empty, we want to run the block that the caller supplied. We want to send in the top disk on this pole as the argument to the block.

```
   aBlock value: (stacks at: aPole) first.
```

The message first asks this OrderedCollection for its top element. The message value: tells a block of unevaluated code to execute and to accept the object that follows (i.e., the top disk) as the value of the block's local variable.*

Some unfamiliar messages are being sent. A tilde followed by an equal sign ~= is the selector for "not equal." It returns true or false,

---

* *LISP* programmers note that evaluating a block is like *(APPLY aBlock (LIST arg))*. Pascal programmers note that it is similar to *aBlock(arg)* where *aBlock* is a parametric procedure.

and these booleans understand the message & to be logical "and." Every OrderedCollection (stack) understands the message isEmpty. It also returns a boolean that understands the message not.

So that you can see how topsOtherThan:do: is used, here again is the code for decide:

```
decide
    "use the last disk moved (oldDisk) to find a new disk to move
       (currentDisk) and a disk to put it on top of (destinationDisk)"
    self topsOtherThan: oldDisk do: [:movingDisk |
       movingDisk hasLegalMove ifTrue:
          ["remember the disk upon which to move"
          destinationDisk ← movingDisk bestMove.
          ↑ movingDisk   "return the disk that moves"]].
```

When topsOtherThan:do: is running, aBlock is the entire piece of code in square brackets, and the result of the expression (stacks at: aPole) first is stored into movingDisk just before the block executes. The "return" statement inside the block, ↑ movingDisk, causes the code in the block to terminate. And it causes the methods topsOtherThan:do: and decide to terminate. In decide the ↑ is inside a block, and the block is not evaluated in the original method, but two methods below. When the return is executed, it exits all procedures until it encounters the one in which the ↑ symbol actually appears (Chapter 3 of the Blue Book).

The code for polesOtherThan:do: is very similar to topsOther-Than:do:.

```
polesOtherThan: thisDisk do: aBlock
    "Evaluate the block of code using the top disk on each of the other
       two poles. If a pole is empty, use the mockDisk for that pole."
    1 to: 3 do: [:aPole |
    "Want a pole other than the pole of thisDisk"
    (aPole ~= thisDisk pole) ifTrue:
       [(stacks at: aPole) isEmpty ifTrue:
          ["If the pole is empty, use a mock disk"
          aBlock value: (mockDisks at: aPole) "execute the block"]
       ifFalse:
          ["else use the top disk"
          aBlock value: (stacks at: aPole) first "execute the block"]]]
```

If a pole has no disks, the value we supply to the block is different. We index the proper mock disk from the array, mockDisks, and supply it as the argument to the block.

We are almost done with this example. Please remember the Japanese proverb: "Patience is bitter, but its fruit is sweet." In the hanoi method, after we decide which disk to move and transfer it from one pole to another, we must give the disk that moved a chance to update its internal state. We send the currentDisk the message moveUpon:. Besides updating the disk, moveUpon: controls the animation. The only thing we want to do differently than HanoiDisk did is to set previousPole. We will write a method called moveUpon: in HanoiDiskRules, but we don't really want to override the old version. We want to call the old version, and then execute another statement. In Smalltalk, the reserved word super allows one to call a message in a higher class despite its being redefined in the subclass.

```
moveUpon: destination
    "This disk just moved. Record the new pole and tell the user."
    previousPole ← pole.
    "Run the version of moveUpon: defined in class HanoiDisk."
    super moveUpon: destination.
```

At the end of the main loop in hanoi, we test if the game is finished.

```
allOnOneTower
    "Return true if all of the disks are on one tower."
    stacks do: [:each | each size = howMany ifTrue: [ ↑ true]].
    ↑ false
```

All kinds of collections in Smalltalk understand the message do:. For each element in the array stacks, supply that stack as an argument to the block. The code in the block tests whether the stack has all of the disks on it. When one stack has all the disks, we are done.

The rest of the code is concerned with initializing the data structures. In class TowerByRules we modify setUpDisks slightly:

```
setUpDisks      | disk displayBox |
    "Create the disks and set up the poles."
    "Make self global for debugging. Later, the user can examine the data
        structures by selecting Hanoi inspect and choosing do it."
    Smalltalk at: #Hanoi put: self.
    "Tell all disks what game they are in and set disk thickness and gap"
    HanoiDiskRules new whichTowers: self.
    displayBox ← 20@100 corner: 380@320.
    Display white: displayBox.
    Display border: displayBox width: 2.
```

```
"The poles are an array of three stacks. Each stack is an
    OrderedCollection."
stacks ← (Array new: 3) collect: [:each | OrderedCollection new].
howMany to: 1 by: −1 do: [:size |
    disk ← HanoiDiskRules new width: size pole: 1. "Create a disk"
    (stacks at: 1) addFirst: disk.     "Push it onto a stack"
    disk invert     "show on the screen"].

"When a pole has no disk on it, one of these mock disks acts as a bottom
    disk. A moving disk will ask a mock disk its width and pole number"
mockDisks ← Array new: 3.
1 to: 3 do: [:index |
    mockDisks at: index put: (HanoiDiskRules new width: 1000 pole: index)].
"On the first move, look for another disk (a real one) to move."
oldDisk ← mockDisks at: 3.
```

This method is identical to the one in class AnimatedTowerOf-
Hanoi, except for the name of the class of the disks (HanoiDiskRules)
and an extra statement at the beginning and one at the end. The statement

```
Smalltalk at: #Hanoi put: self.
```

creates a global variable Hanoi in Smalltalk, the dictionary of global
variables. This does not help our program, but it allows us to get our
hands on the object that represents the game. After the program has
finished, or if it stops in the middle with an error, we can see the state
of the game by executing Hanoi inspect. An inspector window allows
you to see inside an object and change the values of its instance variables. Inspectors are covered in Chapter 8 of the User's Guide.

At the start of the Tower of Hanoi program, oldDisk must be a disk
that is not on stack number one. This is because the program looks for
a disk to move that is on top of a pole other than oldDisk's pole. However, all real disks *are* on stack number one! Assigning oldDisk a mock
disk that thinks it is on pole number three does the trick.

```
oldDisk ← mockDisks at: 3.
```

In class HanoiDiskRules, we need to define the message that ini-
tializes a disk (a disk in the game that is, not a disk in a disk drive).

```
width: size pole: whichPole
    "Invoke width:pole: in the superclass"
    super width: size pole: whichPole.
    previousPole ← 1.
```

We use **super** to do exactly what HanoiDisk would have done, and then set previousPole to 1.

DEFINING THE CLASSES HanoiDiskRules **AND** TowerByRules

That's not writing, that's typing!
TRUMAN CAPOTE COMMENTING ON JACK KEROUAC'S WORK

We are now ready to enter the code we discussed in the previous section. Installing these two classes is exactly like installing the two classes in the last chapter. Here is the definition of HanoiDiskRules:

```
HanoiDisk subclass: #HanoiDiskRules
   instanceVariableNames: ' previousPole '
   classVariableNames: ''
   poolDictionaries: ''
   category: 'Kernel-Objects'
```

The class comment is simple:

```
previousPole--number of the pole this disk was on previously
```

The protocols for HanoiDiskRules are

```
('access' )
('moving' )
```

In the **access** protocol:

```
width
   "Return the size of this disk"
   ↑ width
```

```
width: size pole: whichPole
   "Invoke width:pole: in the superclass"
   super width: size pole: whichPole.
   previousPole ← 1.
```

In the protocol **moving**:

bestMove | secondBest |
    "If self can move two places, which is best? Return the top disk of
        the pole that this disk has not been on recently."
    TheTowers polesOtherThan: self do: [:targetDisk |
        width < targetDisk width ifTrue:
        [secondBest ← targetDisk.
        targetDisk pole = previousPole ifFalse: [↑ targetDisk]]].
    ↑ secondBest "as a last resort, return a pole it was on recently"

Confirm that polesOtherThan:do: is a new message.

hasLegalMove
    "Do either of the other two poles have a top disk large enough for
        this disk to rest on?"
    TheTowers polesOtherThan: self do: [:targetDisk |
        "when a pole has no disk, targetDisk is a mock disk with infinite width"
        width < targetDisk width ifTrue: [↑ true]].
    ↑ false

---

moveUpon: destination
    "This disk just moved. Record the new pole and tell the user."
    previousPole ← pole.
    "Run the version of moveUpon: defined in class HanoiDisk."
    super moveUpon: destination.

Now define the other new class and install its comment and protocols.

AnimatedTowerOfHanoi subclass: #TowerByRules
    instanceVariableNames: 'oldDisk currentDisk destinationDisk'
    classVariableNames: ''
    poolDictionaries: ''
    category: 'Kernel-Objects'

And its comment:

An object of this class represents the game. It holds an array of stacks that
hold disks. It also keeps track of which disk just moved and which disk
should move next. The new instance variables are
    oldDisk--the disk that was moved last time
    currentDisk--we are considering moving this disk
    destinationDisk--and putting it on top of this disk

Under **protocols**, let's divide the messages into two groups:

('initialize')
('moves')

There are two messages in the **initialize** protocol. Be sure to select **initialize** in area C before typing in a method.

```
hanoi
    "Ask the user how many disks, set up the game, and move disks until
        we are done."
    howMany ← (FillInTheBlank request: 'Please type the number of
disks in the tower, and <cr>') asNumber.
    self setUpDisks.     "create the disks and stacks"
    "Iterate until all disks are on one tower again."
    ["decide which to move and also set destinationDisk"
    currentDisk ← self decide.
    "remove the disk and put it on the new pole"
    (stacks at: currentDisk pole) removeFirst.
    (stacks at: destinationDisk pole) addFirst: currentDisk.
    "tell the disk where it is now"
    currentDisk moveUpon: destinationDisk.
    oldDisk ← currentDisk.     "get ready for the next move"
    self allOnOneTower] whileFalse.     "test if done"

    " (TowerByRules new) hanoi "
```

Copy this method from AnimatedTowerOfHanoi and make the underlined changes:

```
setUpDisks     | disk displayBox |
    "Create the disks and set up the poles."
    "Make self global for debugging. Later, the user can examine the data
        structures by selecting Hanoi inspect and choosing do it."
    Smalltalk at: #Hanoi put: self.
    "Tell all disks what game they are in and set disk thickness and gap"
    HanoiDiskRules new whichTowers: self.
    displayBox ← 20@100 corner: 380@320.
    Display white: displayBox.
    Display border: displayBox width: 2.
    "The poles are an array of three stacks. Each stack is an
        OrderedCollection."
    stacks ← (Array new: 3) collect: [:each | OrderedCollection new].
    howMany to: 1 by: −1 do: [:size |
        disk ← HanoiDiskRules new width: size pole: 1. "Create a disk"
        (stacks at: 1) addFirst: disk.     "Push it onto a stack"
        disk invert     "show on the screen"].
```

"When a pole has no disk on it, one of these mock disks acts as a bottom
   disk. A moving disk will ask a mock disk its width and pole number"
mockDisks ← Array new: 3.
1 to: 3 do: [:index |
   mockDisks at: index put: (HanoiDiskRules new width: 1000 pole: index)].
"On the first move, look for another disk (a real one) to move."
<u>oldDisk ← mockDisks at: 3.</u>

Select protocol **moves** and enter four methods.

allOnOneTower
   "Return true if all of the disks are on one tower."
   stacks do: [:each | each size = howMany ifTrue: [↑ true]].
   ↑ false

decide
   "use the last disk moved (oldDisk) to find a new disk to move
      (currentDisk) and a disk to put it on top of (destinationDisk)"
   self topsOtherThan: oldDisk do: [:movingDisk |
      movingDisk hasLegalMove ifTrue:
      ["remember the disk upon which to move"
      destinationDisk ← movingDisk bestMove.
      ↑ movingDisk   "return the disk that moves"]].

Confirm that topsOtherThan:do: is a new message.

polesOtherThan: thisDisk do: aBlock
   "Evaluate the block of code using the top disk on each of the other
      two poles. If a pole is empty, use the mockDisk for that pole."
   1 to: 3 do: [:aPole |
   "Want a pole other than the pole of thisDisk"
   (aPole ~= thisDisk pole) ifTrue:
      [(stacks at: aPole) isEmpty ifTrue:
         ["If the pole is empty, use a mock disk"
         aBlock value: (mockDisks at: aPole) "execute the block"]
      ifFalse:
         ["else use the top disk"
         aBlock value: (stacks at: aPole) first "execute the block"]]]

```
topsOtherThan: thisDisk do: aBlock
    "Evaluate the block of code using the top disk on each of the other
    two poles. If a pole is empty, ignore it. This is for actual disks."
    1 to: 3 do: [:aPole |
        "If the pole does not have thisDisk and is not empty, then
        execute aBlock"
        (aPole ~= thisDisk pole) & ((stacks at: aPole) isEmpty not) ifTrue:
        [aBlock value: (stacks at: aPole) first "execute the block"]]
```

Now lets see the program run with the new algorithm. Look at the hanoi method in the **initialize** category in TowerByRules. Select and execute:

(TowerByRules new) hanoi

We programmers tend to think of the algorithm as everything, but there are lots of things to write in a program, besides the actual algorithm. If you've ever tried to program an algorithm that you already knew on a system you didn't know, you quickly discover the "other stuff." We did a somewhat unusual thing in this chapter: we kept everything from the AnimatedTowerOfHanoi example except the algorithm. Several different aspects of Smalltalk helped us replace the algorithm easily. Because we divided the problem cleanly into objects, many of the old data structures were right for the new algorithm (stacks, howMany, and a disk's name, width, pole, and rectangle). Because Smalltalk sends messages between objects, and because the methods that answer those messages are short and single-purposed, many of our example's methods for input, output, and initialization did not need to change when the algorithm changed. Because Smalltalk allows subclasses to inherit structure and behavior from their parent classes, we did not have to make a copy of the entire class HanoiDisk in order to change it. The definition of our new class, HanoiDiskRules, contains only the changes from the old class. As programmers, we spend much of our time changing existing programs. Many of the features in the Smalltalk-80 system are there to support the following principle (often expressed by Peter Deutsch): When you make a conceptual change, you should only have to modify the parts of the program that embody that concept.

ON YOUR OWN

FINDING WHAT YOU NEED

*The best effect of any book is that
it excites the reader to self activity.*

THOMAS CARLYLE

Before you further extend your program, write other programs, and become an expert at the Smalltalk system, you should know a few hints. As we said before, each Smalltalk class is like a "module" or "package," and the entire Smalltalk-80 system is like a large subroutine library. The browser is an information retrieval window into that library. Classes are grouped into "categories" to make them easier to find. Some categories contain classes which are related by all being subclasses of a particular class (the subclasses of Number in **Numeric-Numbers**, for example). In general, a common purpose or a common use unites the classes in a category, and while some of them are subclasses of each other, many are not.

You are not expected to memorize where to find classes, or which classes respond to which messages. However, the **Kernel-**, **Numeric-**, and **Collections-** categories are so important that we urge you to read Chapters 6 through 14 in the Blue Book to learn what these classes do and where to find them in the browser.

When you sit down to "write a program" in the conventional sense, you will almost always define a new class. When you add functionality to the system, or modify the behavior of the system, you will usually add methods to existing classes. Another common practice is to make a subclass of an existing class, solely to override a couple of its methods, being confident that you won't interfere with the normal functioning of that class.

As a Smalltalk programmer you rarely just sit down and write code. A common practice is to find another part of the system that does something very similar to the thing you want to do. You read that code, copy it into the method you are writing, and modify it to your specific needs. There are several techniques for finding a piece of code when you see its actions in another part of the system. Let's try some of these techniques. Suppose you know the name of class String, but don't know which category it is in. Enter area E of a browser or the transcript. Type String category and choose **print it** from the middle-button menu. The answer, Collections-Text, is inserted in the text just after your selection, as shown in Figure 7.1. (You will need to **cancel** the change to the text before the system will let you try the other examples here.)

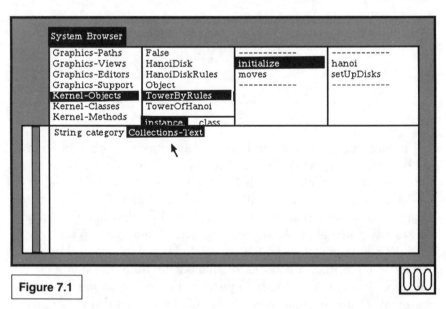

Figure 7.1

Another technique to find a piece of code is to interrupt the system when it is doing the thing you want to find out about. Suppose you can run the Tower of Hanoi animation, but don't know where to find the code in the browser. You can start the hanoi animation and then type *control C* (*Command period* on a Macintosh). A new window

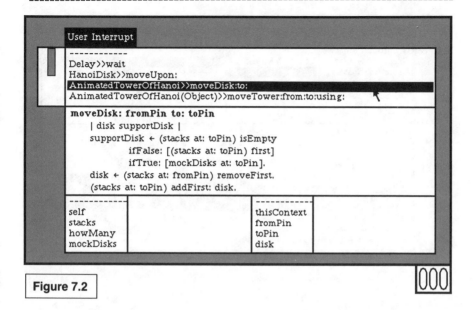

Figure 7.2

will appear. If you open the error window by choosing **debug** from the middle-button menu, you will see the execution stack in the upper pane. You can find the code you are after by clicking on the various message names in the upper pane (see Figure 7.2). The debugger is extremely useful, but we haven't the space to cover it here. See Chapter 19 of the User's Guide for complete instructions.

When you are reading a specific piece of code, you will want to know more about the variables and messages you find. Suppose you are looking at the code for the method hanoi in the browser. You see a reference to something called FillInTheBlank, but you have no idea what it is. Select FillInTheBlank and then choose **explain** from the middle-button menu. The system will tell you about the thing you have selected. **explain** works for any single token in a method, including variables, selectors, pieces of selectors, and all punctuation. (**explain** has been taken out of Apple's Level 0 image to save space.) Sometimes the description includes a Smalltalk expression, which is meant to be evaluated, as shown in Figure 7.3.

When you say **do it**, the system asks you to frame a new browser that is specialized to the variable or class. You can now explore class FillInTheBlank and see what messages it responds to (see Figure 7.4).

Suppose that you are exploring a class and are trying to discover what an instance variable in that class does. For example, take the instance variable stacks in the class AnimatedTowersOfHanoi. In area B of the browser, select AnimatedTowersOfHanoi. The first thing to do is to choose **comment** and read it. If the comment is not very illuminat-

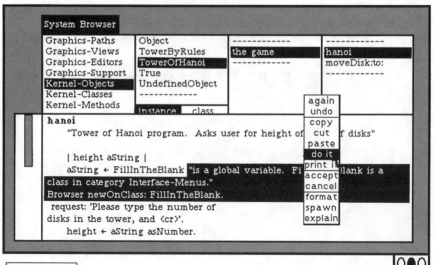

Figure 7.3

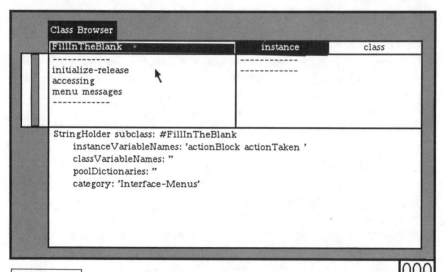

Figure 7.4

ing, you may want to see every place in the system that the variable stacks is used. In area B, choose **inst var refs** from the middle-button menu. The browser puts up a new menu that lists the instance variables by name. Click on **stacks**, as shown in Figure 7.5.

The system asks you to frame a window for a new browser on a list of methods. This browser shows you all the methods in the system in which the instance variable stacks appears. You can see the method in the lower pane by clicking on its name in the upper pane. You can

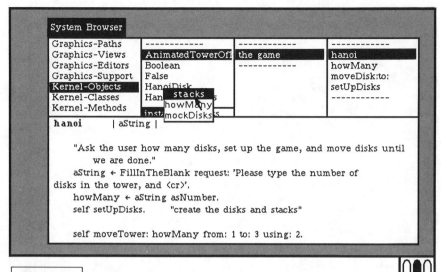

Figure 7.5

make changes to the method and **accept** it without leaving this method list window. Whenever you need to change all uses of a variable systematically, this kind of window is ideal (see Figure 7.6).

The item **class var refs** in the middle-button menu is exactly like **inst var refs**. It shows you all the places a particular class variable is used.

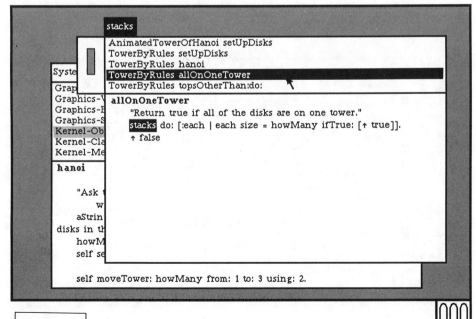

Figure 7.6

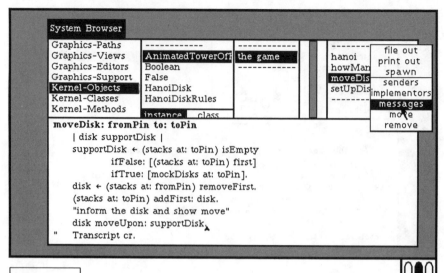

Figure 7.7

As you read code, you will often come across an unfamiliar message name. Suppose you are looking at the method moveDisk:to: in area E of the browser, and you notice the selector addFirst:. To see the code that implements addFirst:, go to area D and choose **messages** from the middle-button menu (see Figure 7.7).

A new menu will appear with the names of all messages sent from moveDisk:to: (see Figure 7.8). Click on addFirst:.

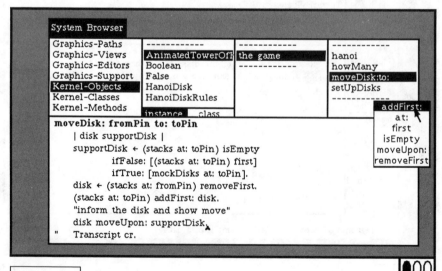

Figure 7.8

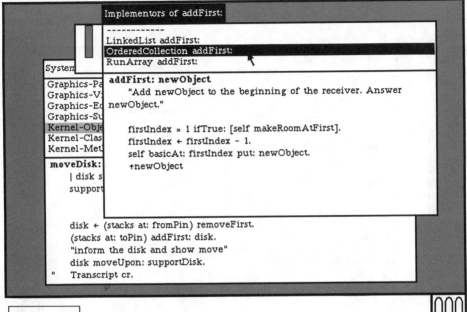

Figure 7.9

The system will ask you to frame a special browser containing all the methods in the entire system that are named addFirst: (see Figure 7.9).

Notice that the classes LinkedList and RunArray have specialized responses to the message addFirst:. Suppose you want to see another call on addFirst: in order to really understand how it works. Click on OrderedCollection addFirst:, as shown in Figure 7.9. Now hold down the middle-button in the upper part of the window, and choose **senders** (see Figure 7.10).

senders finds all methods in the system which call addFirst:, and the system asks you to frame a window in which to show them (see Figure 7.11).

The list of senders of addFirst: includes calls on all three of the implementations (definitions in different classes), since the system cannot determine the class of the receiver of the message until runtime. Any message list menu, like area D of the browser, allows you to choose **messages** and **senders** from its middle-button menu. See the Inquiry section in the System Workspace window for some useful ready-made templates for searching the system. (Also see Section 5.4 and Chapter 10 of the User's Guide.)

In the Tower of Hanoi program, the method move-Tower:from:to:using: is not in the class AnimatedTowersOfHanoi. It is inherited from Object because TowerOfHanoi is a subclass of Object and

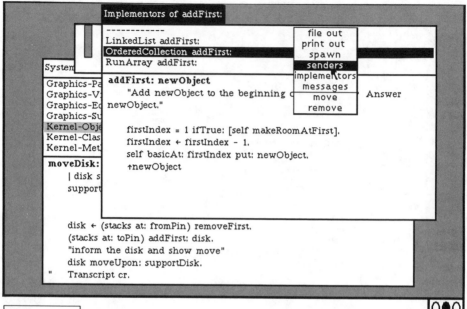

Figure 7.10

AnimatedTowersOfHanoi is a subclass of TowerOfHanoi. When you are exploring a class, it is valuable to see the subclass relationships. Enter the browser, and make sure AnimatedTowersOfHanoi is selected in area

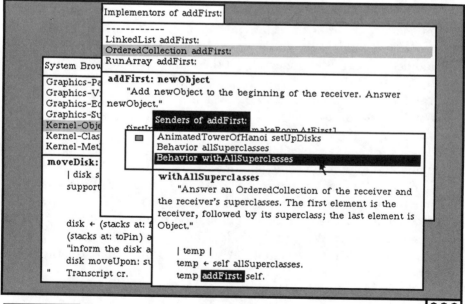

Figure 7.11

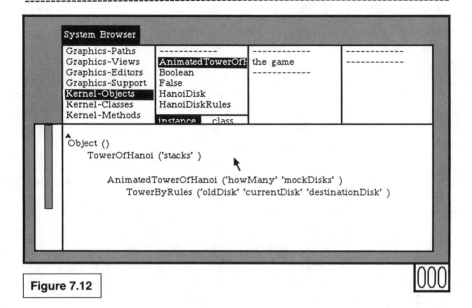

Figure 7.12

B. Choose **hierarchy** from the middle-button menu. Area E will change into a picture of the subclass hierarchy (see Figure 7.12).

A system with overlapping windows and the ability to copy code from one window to another allows you to adopt a style of work different from a "full screen" editor on a character display. While writing code you may want three browsers (or spawned windows) open at once. One contains the method you are currently writing, one is for looking at the rest of your own code (the methods you just wrote), and one is for browsing around the system to find things to copy or use.

To open a new browser, move the cursor so that it is in the gray area between windows, and choose **browser** from the middle-button pop-up menu. (As you might guess, **file list**, **workspace**, **system transcript**, and **system workspace** on the same menu create new instances of other windows. If you ever accidentally hit the right button of the mouse and close a window unintentionally, you can use these menu items to get back another window of the same kind.)

Since this book is a slim introductory volume, we have not covered a number of important topics in Smalltalk. Here is a brief list of topics, so that you will experience "name recognition" when you hear about them later, or see them in the Smalltalk system.

- You can send a message to a class, instead of to one of its instances. Messages to a class are most often used to create instances or to ask about class-wide information. Some examples we have seen are Array new:, FillInTheBlank request:, and Character value:. You

can view class messages by clicking on the word **class** at the
bottom of area B in the browser. See Chapter 5 of the Blue
Book.

- Besides local variables and instance variables, there are three
  other kinds of variables. Global variables are stored in a dictionary called Smalltalk. You are able to mention the name of a
  class in a method because all classes are stored under their names
  as globals. The globals that are not classes (and thus cannot be
  found in the browser) are listed in the Globals section of the
  System Workspace window. We have seen "class variables," such
  as DiskGap in HanoiDisk. They are common to a particular class,
  its subclasses, and all of their instances. Pool variables are a
  particularly obscure kind, shared by classes that are not related
  by subclassing. See Chapter 3 of the Blue Book.
- We have not explained subclasses, superclasses, and inheritance in their full glory. See Chapter 4 of the Blue Book. In
  some versions of Smalltalk, a class can even inherit behavior
  from more than one direct superclass.
- Inspector windows are useful because they let you look inside
  objects. You can send the message inspect to any object, or you
  can choose **inspect** from the middle-button menu in any window that is a list of objects. Lists of objects appear in the bottom
  panes of the debugger and also in inspect windows. Once in an
  inspector, you can change the values of the instance variables of
  the object.
- The System Workspace is simply a window full of text. You may
  have used it already to bring in source code from a file. The text
  in the window is a series of templates for commonly used actions.
  You edit an expression to customize it, select it, and then choose
  do it or **print it**. (**do it** executes the code and **print it** both executes the code and inserts the result in line.) The commands are
  for interacting with an external operating system (the Files section), saving your work (fileOutChanges), searching the system
  (the Inquiry section), managing Smalltalk's global resources (Display and Processor), and making measurements (coreLeft, spyOn:).
  See Section 6.3 and the System Workspace Index of the User's
  Guide.
- "Projects" are multiple screens that you can flip among. They
  are useful for separating different projects you are working on.
  You can set up a screen full of windows for each project you are
  working on (such as writing a paper, reading your mail, and
  designing a new browser), and then flip quickly between them.
  See Chapter 4 of the User's Guide.

- There are four different tools for managing programs you have written. You can save the entire state of your system by choosing **save** or **quit** from the middle-button menu in the gray space between windows. You can write out the source code for individual classes (**file out** in the middle-button menu in area B of the browser), or all your changes (in the System Workspace). Or, you can use the Change-Management Browser for a high degree of control over your changes.
- Yes, we even offer insurance! If your machine crashes, you can always get the text of all the methods you wrote before the crash by restarting the system and then executing (Smalltalk recover: 10000). For the specifics, read Chapter 23 of the User's Guide.

WHAT IS OBJECT-ORIENTED PROGRAMMING, REALLY?

The series of example programs we have built to solve the Tower of Hanoi puzzle represents a spectrum of style. The first version (in class Object) was simply a transcription of the normal recursive solution. Even though the Smalltalk version used objects and sent messages to them, it was not an example of object-oriented programming. It is perfectly possible to write the exact analog of FORTRAN programs in Smalltalk. When we divided the problem up into disks and a game-wide object, the algorithm became more object-oriented. The algorithm used in AnimatedTowerOfHanoi and HanoiDisk was not totally object-oriented, however, because the recursive version could compute the solution without using the stacks or the data in the disks! The rule-based algorithm really uses its data structures. In class Tower-ByRules and HanoiDiskRules, the objects use their data structures and decide where to move by sending messages to each other. In the last chapter we wrote a program that is truly object-oriented.

The idea of modular code is well established in computer science, but it alone does not make a program object-oriented. In a language other than Smalltalk, the routines that deal with a specific function are packaged together. The data structures, however, are usually global. In a typical text editor, it is common for all routines that actually modify the text to be in one package, but usually the data structures that hold the actual text are global. Any other routine *could* reach in and change text. In real-world systems, "reaching in the back door" to modify the data structure is quite common. Suppose segments of text in the text editor have "dirty bits" associated with them. This bit needs to be turned on every time a piece of text is modified or the changes will not be saved to disk. The only way a programmer can be sure that the dirty bit is being set every time it should be is to search the entire program for places that write into the textual data structures. In Smalltalk, if an object owns some data, no other object can reach that data without sending a message to the owner. If an instance of class **Text** needs to enforce the setting of dirty bits, the programmer must search only the methods in class **Text**.

Let's get away from talking about protection of data. Imagine that every fragment of program and every piece of data are floating together in space. Now imagine pieces of string between code and the data it uses, and between segments of code that are used together or perform a similar function. Let's move everything around until the total amount of string is the smallest. Clustered around each data structure are the routines that use it. Natural divisions in the code become apparent. When a problem is segmented into classes along natural boundaries, the resulting program is beautiful. Dividing a problem up into objects is a process of putting things where they belong.

The most important part of object-oriented programming is not any technical advantage it gives, but the fact that it crosses a threshold of perception. When we put all of the information associated with a disk into class **HanoiDisk**, we didn't just clean up the code in **AnimatedTowerOfHanoi**. We allowed ourselves to think of that body of information and action as a single unit, namely, "a disk." We are used to perceiving the world around us as made up of "objects," and our brains arrange information into "chunks." By using objects in a programming language, we can tap into an existing convention. Thinking of an algorithm in terms of objects makes it easier to understand. This ease of understanding often comes not from the details of the class you are working on, but from *not* having to think about the rest of the program. When you are working inside one class, you are largely safe from the side effects and complexities of parts of your program outside that class.

Dividing a problem up into objects and defining actions that are "natural" for those objects actually make programs simpler. When the actions of an object are divided into the right kinds of "chunks," we can think and write code at a higher level. We know that the methods we call from the high-level code are correct, because they match the way we think about the problem. When that trust exists, we make fewer mistakes. We carry around less tension about whether the subordinate procedures are doing the right thing. Programs are uncluttered and easier to maintain.

In Smalltalk, the overhead of sending a message is small. Since sending a message is the only thing you can do in a piece of Smalltalk code, it has been optimized. An average method has ten to fifty message sends in it. If an expression keeps cropping up over and over in a program, it probably deserves to be a separate method. The goal in Smalltalk is to make creating a new method as easy as possible. Writing a new method and calling it in the original program should be easier than defining a new procedure in Pascal. Declarations and preambles are very short in Smalltalk, and you can edit, run, and debug without changing environments. Processing a file through a compiler after typing a program into it introduces unnecessary complexity. Why should a file system come between you and your program? Messages and methods are meant to be lightweight and quick to install. In Smalltalk, compiling a method and linking it into the system take only a few seconds, as opposed to several minutes in a "batch-processed" Pascal or C system where many modules may have to be recompiled.

Some of the signs of non-object-oriented programming are too many loops and too much indexing of multi-level data structures. Compare the method for **bestMove** in **HanoiDiskRules** (shown below) with the equivalent code in a style that is not object oriented.

```
bestMove     | secondBest |
   "If self can move two places, which is best? Return the top disk of
     the pole that this disk has not been on recently."
   TheTowers polesOtherThan: self do: [:targetDisk |
     width < targetDisk width ifTrue:
      [secondBest ← targetDisk.
       targetDisk pole = previousPole ifFalse: [ ↑ targetDisk]]].
   ↑ secondBest "as a last resort, return a pole it was on recently"
```

If we rewrite this program in the style of a traditional language, the code becomes bulky and hard to understand. polesOtherThan:do: is not written as a separate procedure, but this is probably how most Pascal programmers would write it.

```
bestMove: movingDisk on: currentPole
   "If movingDisk can move to two places, which is best? Return
     the pole that the disk fits on and has not been on recently."
   1 to: 3 do: [:targetPole | "each other pole"
     targetPole ~= currentPole ifTrue:
      ["Not the current pole"
       (stacks at: targetPole) isEmpty
       ifTrue: ["We know it fits on an empty pole"
         secondBest ← targetPole.
```

```
                "Is this the pole we just came from? Look in an array of
                    previousPoles"
                targetPole = (previousPoles at: movingDisk) ifFalse:
                    [↑ targetPole "the best"]]
            ifFalse: ["a real disk is on top"
                "compare the widths"
                movingDisk < ((stacks at: targetPole) at:
                        (stackTops at: targetPole))
                    ifTrue: ["it fits"
                        "Is this the pole we just came from?
                            Look in an array of previousPoles"
                        targetPole = (previousPoles at: movingDisk) ifFalse:
                            [↑ targetPole "the best"]]]]].
    ↑ secondBest        "as a last resort, return the pole it was on recently"
```

Good design and clean code are not the sole province of Smalltalk. It is possible to write extremely beautiful code in other languages, as well as terrible code in Smalltalk. Smalltalk even has its own particular kinds of brier patches. (Look at the code in Behavior, ClassDescription, and Class that runs when you accept a class definition for an existing class in which you rename its instance variables.) The designers of Smalltalk believe that you already know what makes a good design and clean code. Smalltalk tries to encourage you to follow your instincts for good design.

Now that you've successfully created a truly object-oriented animated program, consider yourself an Official Level One Smalltalk Programmer! Perhaps the next step is to add some bells and whistles to your animated Tower of Hanoi program. Appendix 4 has seven suggestions (four bells and three whistles), with Appendix 5 hinting at the answers and Appendix 6 just giving them away. If you want to learn even more about Smalltalk, we suggest going through the User's Guide (the bit-editor is really fun). You might then read Part I of the Blue Book, and try the FinancialHistory example in Appendix I of the User's Guide. You've had a taste of Smalltalk, and we hope to have whetted your appetite. Bon appétit!

APPENDIX 1

THE SMALLTALK TEXT EDITOR

To replace a passage of text, select it by pressing the left button at the beginning of the passage and releasing it at the end. Then type the new passage. The first keystroke will delete the old passage.

The middle-button pop-up menu contains the commands used to edit text. This menu is available wherever you can type text.

again   do the last **paste** again, but in a new place. Find the next occurrence of the text that was pasted over last time. Replace that text.

undo   undo the last editing action (only works one command back and only if the selection has not moved).

copy   remember the text that is currently selected.

cut   remove the text that is currently selected.

paste   replace the selection with what was last cut, copied, or typed.*

do it   treat the current selection as Smalltalk code and evaluate it.

print it   treat the current selection as Smalltalk code, run it, and insert the result after the selection.

* Macintosh users should note that paste will not paste in the last thing typed. It must have been cut or copied. In this respect, the text editor in Apple's version of Smalltalk has been modified to be like the Macintosh text editor.

accept   compile, link, and load the method (or class definition) in this window.

cancel   redisplays the text as it was at the time of the last **accept** (undoes all edits since the last **accept**).

format   pretty print the text for this method; in other words indent the program so it is easy to read. If you like the new form, choose **accept** afterwards. Does not work if you have changed the text since the last **accept**.

spawn   creates a new browser, just for this method.

explain   inserts an explanation of the single thing that is selected. It has trouble if more than one "thing" is selected.

For more detail on the text editor, see Chapter 3 of the User's Guide.

APPENDIX 2

HOW TO TALK TO YOURSELF WHEN READING SMALLTALK

As we mentioned above, some people feel the need to pronounce when writing programs. We have provided a Smalltalkese reading of moveTower:from:to:using: and moveDisk:to:.

```
moveTower: height from: fromPin to: toPin using: usingPin
    "Recursive procedure to move the disk at a height from one
        pin to another pin using a third pin"
    (height > 0) ifTrue: [
        self moveTower: (height − 1) from: fromPin to: usingPin using: toPin.
        self moveDisk: fromPin to: toPin.
        self moveTower: (height − 1) from: usingPin to: toPin using: fromPin]

    "This comment gives an example of how to run this program. Select
    the following and choose 'do it' from the middle-button menu.
        (Object new) moveTower: 3 from: 1 to: 3 using: 2          "
```

The method for move-tower-from-to-using. The arguments are height, from-pin, to-pin, and using-pin. (A recursive procedure to move the disk at a height from one pin to another pin using a third pin.) Height is greater than zero, if true, send yourself move-tower with height minus one, from from-pin, to using-pin, using to-pin. Send yourself move-disk from from-pin to to-pin. Send yourself move-tower with height minus one, from using-pin, to to-pin, using from-pin. Return self ("return self" is the "amen" of Smalltalk). This benediction is implicitly at the end of every method.

```
moveDisk: fromPin to: toPin
    "Move a disk from a pin to another pin. Print the results in the
        transcript window"
    Transcript cr.
    Transcript show: (fromPin printString, ' -> ', toPin printString).
```

The method for move-disk-to. The arguments are from-pin and to-pin. (Move a disk from a pin to another pin. Print the results in the transcript window.) Transcript carriage return. Transcript show from-pin's print string, concatenated with the string for a little arrow, concatenated with to-pin's print string. (This program is not actually doing anything about moving the disks!) Return self (Amen).

APPENDIX 3

METHODS MISSING FROM THE APPLE LEVEL 0 IMAGE

Early versions of the Level 0 Smalltalk system for the Macintosh 512K have some methods missing. The Level 0 system is a cut-down version of Apple's Level 1 system (which is for machines with a megabyte of memory or more). A few classes and many messages were removed to make a small system. The programs in this book happen to use two methods that were taken out, as well as one that was changed. Please follow the directions below to install the missing methods, and then return to defining the method hanoi in Chapter 3.

(1) Enter area A of the browser and scroll to the category **Interface-Browser**. It is above **Kernel-Objects** and is the fourth **Interface-** category. Select **Interface-Browser** by clicking on it.

(2) Select MessageCategoryListView in area B. (Area B may not be wide enough to see all of the name. Of the two names that begin MessageCategoryLi..., select the second one.)

(3) In area C, the system automatically selects **As yet unclassified**. Choose list: in area D.

(4) In area E, all you need to do is add the word self and a space to the beginning of the last line. The change is underlined below.

```
list: anArray
    "Refer to the comment in ListView|list:"

    super list: anArray.
    (anArray ~= nil and: [anArray size = 1]) ifTrue:
       [selection ← 1.
       self controller preSelectModeSelection: 1]
```

(5) Choose **accept** from the middle-button menu. (You may be wondering what you just fixed. Notice that in Step 3 above, the single item in area C was selected automatically. The bug we just fixed was introduced when that feature was added. When we create a new browser window, as is done in Chapter 4, this code tries to select the only item in area C before the variable controller is initialized. Sending the message self controller instead gets us the same variable, but the code happens to check if it is uninitialized. But wait, we don't yet know enough about Smalltalk to make sense of this.)

(6) Enter area A of the browser and select the category **Interface-Menus**. It is the category above **Interface-Browser**, the one we were just in. Select **Interface-Menus** by clicking on it.

(7) Select FillInTheBlank in area B.

(8) Earlier we said that we would never use the **class** switch in area F of the browser (below area B). Well, now we have to use it just for a moment, and then we will switch it back to **instance**. Move the cursor down from area B to area F and click on **class**.

(9) In area C, the system automatically selects **As yet unclassified**. Look in area D to see if the method request: is there. If it is, you don't have to type it in after all, and can go directly to step 13. Otherwise . . .

(10) In area E, select all the text and replace it with

```
request: messageString
    "Create an instance of FillInTheBlank whose question is mes-
    sageString. Display it centered around the cursor. Return the
    string that the user types and accepts."

self
    request: messageString
    displayAt: Sensor cursorPoint
    centered: true
    action: [:response | response]
    initialAnswer: ".   "<-two single quotes"
    ↑ response
```

(11) In the line before the last line, initialAnswer: ". has two single-quote characters after the colon. Two single quotes in a row is a null String. It is the same thing as (String new: 0). (We also can't resist telling you what this code does. self is the object FillInTheBlank, which is a "class." We will learn about classes in Chapter 4. self is sent the message

request:displayAt:centered:action:initialAnswer:. Because of the block, the local variable response is set as a side effect. In the last line, the method returns the value in the variable response to the caller. We will discuss return in detail later.)

(12) Choose **accept** from the middle-button menu.

(13) Move to area F and click on **instance**. *Be sure to do this!* If you leave the switch on **class**, you won't be able to find things in the browser. Now let's define the other missing method.

(14) Enter area A and scroll to the category **Collections-Text**. It is above the **Interface-** categories and is the fourth **Collections-** category. Select **Collections-Text**.

(15) Select String in area B.

(16) In area C, the system automatically selects **As yet unclassified**. If asNumber is already in area D, you can skip to Step 19.

(17) In area E, select all the text and replace it with

asNumber
    "self is a string with the ASCII characters for some digits.
    Convert the digits to a number and return it."

    ↑ Number readFrom: (ReadStream on: self)

(18) Choose **accept** from the middle-button menu. (Both the Apple Level 0 and Level 1 systems are Xerox License 1 systems. If you have a License 2 system and are reading this section anyway, we must tell you that License 2 has a new name for the message on:. In the code for asNumber, you will find ReadStream onCollection: self instead of ReadStream on: self.)

(19) Scroll back to **Kernel-Objects**. It is below all the **Interface-** categories. Select **Kernel-Objects** in area A, Object in area B, **games** in area C, and continue with the example on page 38 of the text.

APPENDIX 4

EXERCISES

No more training do you require.
Already know you that which you need.
                    YODA in *The Empire Strikes Back*

To get more experience, modify the animated Tower of Hanoi program to add some bells and whistles. Here are a few suggestions. Appendix 5 contains hints to help you, and Appendix 6 gives some example solutions.

(1) The disks in the animated example are black. Change them to gray.

(2) The disks move from one stack to another by moving directly from their old positions to their new places. Change this so that a disk jumps up above its original stack, jumps across to the new stack, and then jumps down to its final position.

(3) Make the animation pause when any mouse button is pressed.

(4) If you try to use more than 7 disks, the largest ones will overlap each other when they are on adjacent poles. Make the width of a disk depend on the number of disks, so the widest disk is always 80 screen dots wide. Similarly, make the height of the disk depend on the number of disks, so that a full stack of disks is as high as the white rectangle on the screen.

(5) When the game is running and the user presses a mouse button, print (in the transcript) which disks are on each of the three poles.

(6a) Use a **Form** instead of a **Rectangle** for the shape of a disk in class HanoiDisk. Color the disk gray and give it a black border that is two screen dots wide. Class **Form** is in the category **Graphics-Display Objects**.

(6b) Use the follow:while: message in class Form to give the disks smooth movement on the screen. The result should be nice-looking disks and smooth animated movement. Make the disks go in straight lines between their locations, or up and over, or in parabolas.

(7) There is a bug in classes HanoiDisk and HanoiDiskRules. If you create two instances of the game, there will be a conflict in setting the value of TheTowers. TheTowers is shared by all instances of HanoiDisk, when it should only be shared by all instances in a single game. Fix this by giving HanoiDisk a new instance variable that performs the same function as TheTowers. If you have done Problem 4, or just in case you will do it later, Thickness will no longer be a constant, and has the same problem. For completeness, turn every class variable (in class HanoiDisk) that is not a constant into an instance variable.

APPENDIX 5

HINTS FOR THE EXERCISES

The answers can be found on the following pages, but don't peek until you have tried using these hints.

(1) The act of drawing the rectangle is controlled in the method invert in class HanoiDisk. The code says:

```
invert
    Display reverse: rectangle
```

The variable rectangle is a simple Rectangle and does not actually have screen bits stored inside it. BitBlt, Smalltalk's universal bit-slinging algorithm, performs several different types of operations (rules), and each goes through a mask to decide what bits to operate on. Base your changes to invert on the definition of reverse:. Find it by using the **messages** command in the middle-button menu of area D of the browser. (Find the code for invert in the browser, then move to area D and hold down the middle button.) The current mask is Form black, which means the whole rectangle. Form gray is also available.

(2) Modify the method moveUpon: in class HanoiDisk. The two new stopping points are (rectangle center x @ 120) and (destination center x @ 120). Split the delay up into three equal parts, one for each place the disk shows on the screen.

(3) You can read the mouse buttons by sending messages to Sensor, an instance of class InputSensor which is found in the category **System-Support**. Adding Sensor waitNoButton to the program will cause it to pause unless (or until) all buttons are up. You might want to look at the other messages in InputSensor to see what else you can do with the mouse.

(4) The width of a disk is controlled by the constant 14 in the next to last line of the method width:pole: in class HanoiDisk. Create a new class variable to hold the width increment, and compute the proper

value for it in whichTowers:. When the program runs with N disks, the largest disk has a width of N times the increment and the smallest is 1 times the increment wide. To make the height of a disk depend on the number of disks, make Thickness in whichTowers: be a function of the number of disks.

(5) As in Problem 3, add a line to moveUpon: in class HanoiDisk. The expression Sensor anyButtonPressed returns true if the user is holding a button down. The object that represents the whole game (TheTowers, an instance of AnimatedTowerOfHanoi) should be given the task of reporting the stacks, because an individual disk in the process of moving itself does not know what disks are on other poles. Define a new message in AnimatedTowerOfHanoi that prints the report in the Transcript.

(6a) A Form is a rectangle of bits that can be pasted on the screen. It knows its own extent (size), but not its location, so we still need the variable rectangle. Add an instance variable so that each disk can hold a Form. Create a Form by saying

Form extent: rectangle extent.

You can use the message fill:rule:mask: to paint bits into a Form. Look in the classes from which Form inherits its behavior to find the message displayOn:at:clippingBox:rule:mask:, and use it for displaying a Form on the screen.

(6b) The first argument to the message follow:while: should be a block of unevaluated code. It must deliver the next point where the upper left corner of the Form should be displayed. The second argument is another block that returns true until the disk reaches its destination. follow:while: assumes that the image of the disk is not on the screen when it starts to move it, and it does not leave the image on the screen at the end (so we have to compensate).

(7) After you have added an instance variable to the definition of HanoiDisk, you need to find all the places where the class variable you are replacing is used. An easy way to do this is to choose **class var refs** from the middle-button menu in area B. The system will ask you to frame a window, and it will list all of the methods that use the variable. You can see the code by clicking on the method name in the upper pane. Once you are looking at the code, you can modify it and **accept** it.

APPENDIX 6

ANSWERS TO THE EXERCISES

(1) Change the method for invert in class HanoiDisk to be

invert
    "Show a disk on the screen by masking an area and reversing it."
    Display fill: rectangle
      rule: Form reverse
      mask: Form gray.

The rectangle is still merged onto the screen using "exclusive or," but this time not all of the bits are changed. Only where the mask is black are bits on the screen reversed. We could have changed this code inside the reverse: method in class DisplayMedium, but since it is used by many parts of the system, all sorts of things (like highlighting in menus) would suddenly behave differently.

    Notice that the modification we have made works for both AnimatedTowerOfHanoi and TowerByRules. The disks used by TowerByRules are instances of class HanoiDiskRules and they inherit the methods for displaying themselves from HanoiDisk.

(2) Change the method for moveUpon: in class HanoiDisk to be

moveUpon: destination
    "This disk just moved. Record the new pole and tell the user."
    pole ← destination pole.
    self invert.
    "straight up"
    rectangle center: (rectangle center x @ 120).
    self invert.
    (Delay forMilliseconds: 100) wait.

```
self invert.
"sideways"
rectangle center: (destination center x @ 120).
self invert.
(Delay forMilliseconds: 100) wait.
self invert.
"straight down to final location"
rectangle center: destination center − (0 @ (Thickness + DiskGap)).
self invert.
(Delay forMilliseconds: 100) wait.
```

(3) When **Sensor** is sent the message **waitNoButton** while a mouse button is pressed, it waits until you let go of the button. Insert this line:

```
Sensor waitNoButton.      "wait if button mouse is being held"
```

between any two statements in **moveUpon:** in HanoiDisk.

(4) Let's make a new variable to hold the difference in width between successive disks. Call it **WidthDelta** and make it shared by all instances of class HanoiDisk.

First select **HanoiDisk** in area B of the browser. From the middle-button menu in area B, choose **definition**. Add the class variable WidthDelta, as shown:

```
Object subclass: #HanoiDisk
    instanceVariableNames: 'name width pole rectangle'
    classVariableNames: 'Thickness TheTowers DiskGap WidthDelta'
    poolDictionaries: ' '
    category: 'Kernel-Objects'
```

When you choose **accept** from the middle-button menu in area E, the system determines that WidthDelta is a new class variable, and adds it.

To use WidthDelta, replace the number 14 in the next to last line of the method width:pole:.

```
rectangle ← 0@0 extent: (size*WidthDelta) @ Thickness.
```

The only hard part of this solution is deciding what values WidthDelta and Thickness should have. The incremental width is equal to 80 divided by the number of disks. The thickness of a disk is the height of the white rectangle (220) divided by the number of disks, minus the space between disks. Here is a completely new version of **whichTowers** in class HanoiDisk:

```
whichTowers: aTowerOfHanoi
    | number |
    "compute the class-wide constants for disks"
    TheTowers ← aTowerOfHanoi.
    number ← TheTowers howMany.
    WidthDelta ← 80 // number.    "the widest disk is 80"
    DiskGap ← 2.
    Thickness ← (220 // number) − DiskGap.    "divide the height up evenly"
```

You can add a little class to this solution by not letting the disks be too thick. The purpose of making the height vary with the number of disks is to keep the top of the stack on the screen when there are lots of disks. When there are only three or four disks, the disks are quite thick and they don't look as good. Changing the last line to

```
Thickness ← ((220 // number) − DiskGap) min: 14.
    "divide the height up evenly, but not too big"
```

limits the thickness to a pleasing 14 screen dots.

(5) Add a new line of code at the end of moveUpon: in class HanoiDisk:

```
Sensor anyButtonPressed ifTrue: [TheTowers report].
"If the button is pressed, ask the whole game to print its state"
```

It is important to put this line at the end of the method because we want to make our report when the state of the disks on the stacks (from which the report will be generated) agrees with the picture on the screen. We pass the task of actually doing the reporting to The-Towers in the form of a new message. Now let's write the code for that new message in class AnimatedTowerOfHanoi:

```
report
    "Show in the Transcript a written report of which disks are on
        which towers"
    | aStack |
    1 to: 3 do: [:index |
        aStack ← stacks at: index.
        Transcript cr.
        Transcript show: 'Tower number ', index printString.
        aStack isEmpty ifTrue: [Transcript show: ' has no disks']
            ifFalse: [
                Transcript show: ' has disks '.
                aStack reverseDo: [:disk |
                    Transcript nextPut: disk name.
                    Transcript space]]].
    Transcript cr.
    Transcript endEntry.    "force it to show"
```

(6a) Add an instance variable called image to class HanoiDisk. Initialize it by adding these lines to the end of width:pole:

```
size >= 1000 ifFalse: [ "a normal disk"
    image ← Form extent: rectangle extent.    "set its size"
    image fill: image boundingBox
        rule: Form over
        mask: Form gray.      "fill in the halftone"
    image borderWidth: 2].      "give it a border 2 dots wide"
```

Use image as a pattern and invert the bits on the screen where the pattern has black bits. Change the method for invert to be

```
invert
    "Show this disk on the screen by inverting the bits where the Form is
    black"
    image displayOn: Display
        at: rectangle origin
        clippingBox: Display boundingBox
        rule: Form reverse
        mask: Form black
```

(6b) This solution is for a straight-line path between the disk's starting and ending positions. We start with the code for moveUpon: as it appeared before you worked any of the other exercises. All we have to do is send the message follow:while: to the disk's image, and insert this between the call on invert and the code for moving the rectangle. We also need to define and initialize the local variables that hold the amount to move at each step and the number of steps completed.

```
moveUpon: destination        | count endPoint increment |
    "This disk just moved. Record the new pole and tell the user."
    pole ← destination pole.
    "Find the increment to move in a straight line path in 16 small steps"
    count ← 0.
    endPoint ← destination center − (0@(thickness + DiskGap)).
    increment ← endPoint − rectangle center // 16.
    "remove the old image"
    self invert.
    "Move along the path. First block is next point, second is end condition."
    image follow: [rectangle moveBy: increment. rectangle origin]
        while: [(count ← count + 1) <= 16].
    "final position"
    rectangle center: endPoint.
    "display at its final position"
    self invert.
```

You can make the disks travel any path you want by varying the code that supplies Points to follow:while:. Try parabolas or semicircles.

(7) Choose class HanoiDisk in area B, and use the menu item **definition** to get its definition into area E. Add instance variables theTowers, thickness, and widthDelta (not capitalized to distinguish them from the class variables). As mentioned in the hint, choose **class var refs** to get a little browser on the methods that use each of the class variables. In each method, replace the class variable with its corresponding new instance variable. After accepting each of these changes, we must make sure the new instance variables are assigned values in every HanoiDisk that is created. To do this, we need to modify setUpDisks in AnimatedTowerOfHanoi. Previously, whichTowers: was called just once in each game to initialize the class variables in HanoiDisk. Instead let's call it once for every disk that is created.

```
setUpDisks      | disk displayBox |
   "Create the disks and set up the poles."
   "Tell all disks what game they are in and set disk thickness and gap"
   displayBox ← 20@100 corner: 380@320.
   Display white: displayBox.
   Display border: displayBox width: 2.
   "The poles are an array of three stacks. Each stack is an
      OrderedCollection."
   stacks ← (Array new: 3) collect: [:each | OrderedCollection new].
   howMany to: 1 by: −1 do: [:size |
      disk ← HanoiDisk new whichTowers: self. "Create a disk"
      disk width: size pole: 1.
      (stacks at: 1) addFirst: disk.      "Push it onto a stack"
      disk invert "show on the screen"].

   "When a pole has no disk on it, one of these mock disks acts as a bottom
      disk. A moving disk will ask a mock disk its width and pole number"
   mockDisks ← Array new: 3.
   1 to: 3 do: [:index |
      disk ← HanoiDisk new whichTowers: self. "Create a disk"
      mockDisks at: index put: (disk width: 1000 pole: index)].
```

Note that we removed the line in which whichTowers: used to appear. We also need to make the same modification to setUpDisks in TowerByRules. (It's not exactly the same modification—we are creating a new instance of HanoiDiskRules instead of a new instance of HanoiDisk.)

Now you can start one game, interrupt it, and start a second game with a different number of disks. The two games interfere with each other only by occupying the same space on the screen; they no longer try to use the same variables.

INDEX

Entries in sans serif type refer to message (or procedure) names; entries in **sans serif boldface** refer to menu commands.